OSPREY COMBAT AIRCRAFT 107

F-105 THUNDERCHIEF MiG KILLERS OF THE VIETNAM WAR

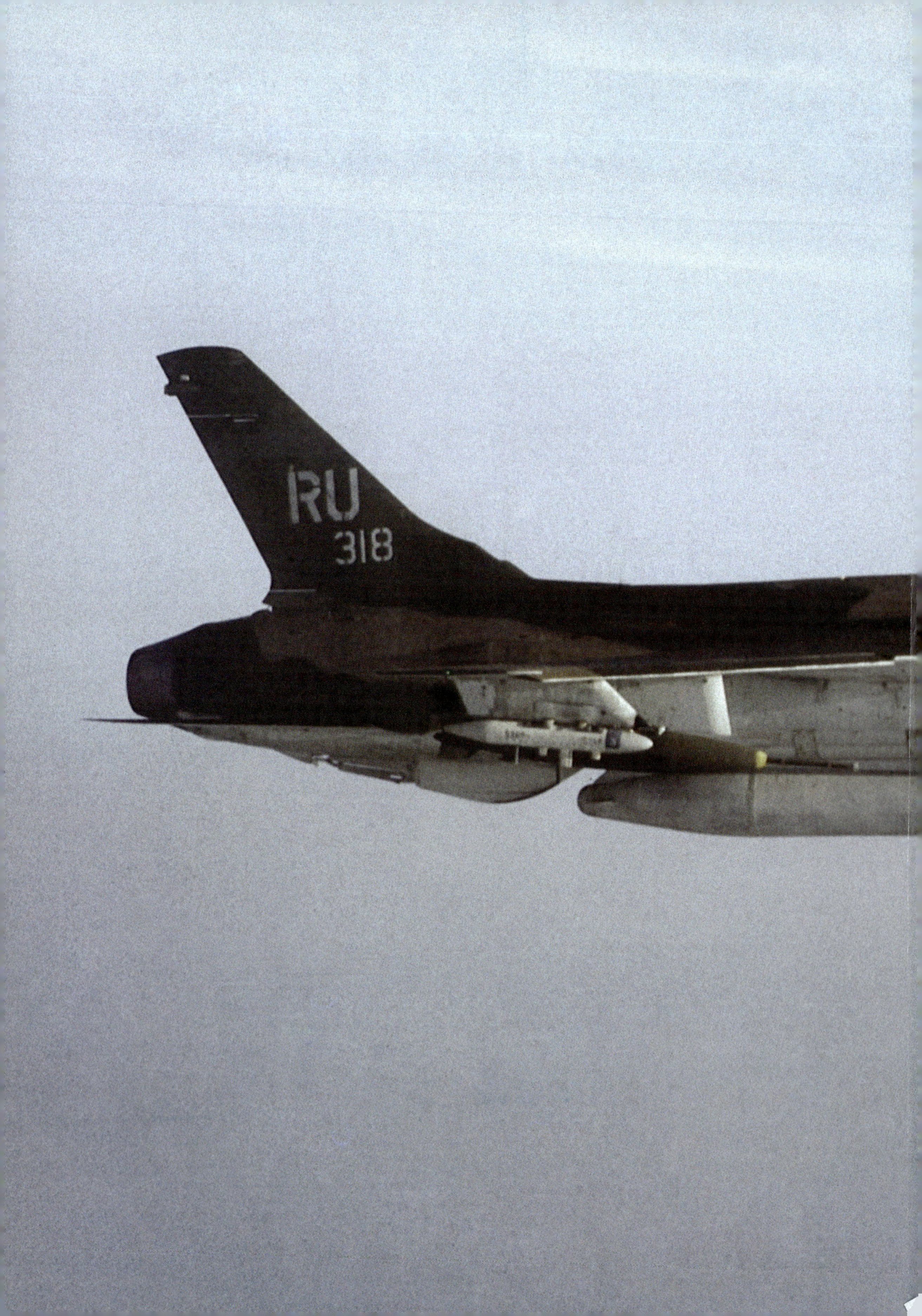
RU
318

SERIES EDITOR TONY HOLMES

OSPREY COMBAT AIRCRAFT • 107

F-105 THUNDERCHIEF MiG KILLERS OF THE VIETNAM WAR

PETER E DAVIES

OSPREY
PUBLISHING

Front Cover
On the afternoon of 19 April 1967 one of the most hair-raising dogfights of the Vietnam War took place after 'Panda' flight, led by Capt William 'Gene' Eskew, had bombed Xuan Mai barracks near Hanoi. Encountering MiG-17s as they left the target, Eskew and his wingman, Capt Paul Seymour, jettisoned their wing tanks and bomb racks ready to engage them, but the enemy fighters escaped. Intercepted by more MiGs over Hoa Binh, 'Panda' re-engaged and both pilots damaged communist fighters.

'Panda' flight then aerial refuelled, after which Eskew offered to return and cover the rescue attempt for downed F-105F crew 'Kingfish 2' since Maj Leo Thorsness, who had fought a one-man battle against MiGs to cover the rescue, had had to leave to refuel. As Eskew led 'Panda' flight towards the downed crewmen four MiG-17s started harassing a pair of A-1E 'Sandy' helicopter escort aircraft, shooting one of them down. Minutes later 'Panda' flight engaged the MiGs at 700 knots and a major low-altitude dogfight ensued. Eskew fired his Sidewinder at one fighter but it failed to detonate. He then turned in behind another MiG that was attacking 'Panda 4' (Capt Paul Hammerle), forcing it away. With an overtake speed of 200 knots, Eskew rapidly closed on the MiG, firing and seeing hits around its canopy. When less than 100 ft from the fighter he pulled up to avoid a collision just as the MiG exploded beneath him. Eskew's fears that his aircraft had sustained major damage proved unfounded, and he went on to attack another MiG-17 that was firing at 'Panda 3', Capt Howard Bodenhamer (Cover artwork by Gareth Hector)

First published in Great Britain in 2014 by Osprey Publishing
PO Box 883, Oxford, OX1 9PL, UK
PO Box 3985, New York, NY 10185-3985, USA

E-mail: info@ospreypublishing.com

Osprey Publishing is part of the Osprey Group

© 2014 Osprey Publishing Limited

All rights reserved. Apart from any fair dealing for the purpose of private study, research, criticism or review, as permitted under the Copyright, Design and Patents Act 1988, no part of this publication may be reproduced, stored in a retrieval system, or transmitted in any form or by any means, electronic, electrical, chemical, mechanical, optical, photocopying, recording or otherwise without prior written permission. All enquiries should be addressed to the publisher.

A CIP catalogue record for this book is available from the British Library

ISBN: 978 1 78200 804 0
PDF e-book ISBN: 978 1 78200 805 7
e-Pub ISBN: 978 1 78200 806 4

Edited by Tony Holmes
Cover Artwork by Gareth Hector
Aircraft Profiles by Jim Laurier
Index by Fionbar Lyons
Originated by PDQ Digital Media Solutions, UK
Printed in China through Asia Pacific Offset Limited

14 15 16 17 18   10 9 8 7 6 5 4 3 2 1

Osprey Publishing is supporting the Woodland Trust, the UK's leading woodland conservation charity, by funding the dedication of trees.

www.ospreypublishing.com

CONTENTS

CHAPTER ONE
THUNDERCHIEF 6

CHAPTER TWO
'THUDS' FIGHT BACK 24

CHAPTER THREE
FRANTIC FIGHTS 38

CHAPTER FOUR
1967 – MiG MAYHEM 61

CHAPTER FIVE
MAY MASSACRE 77

APPENDICES 92
COLOUR PLATES COMMENTARY 93
INDEX 95

CHAPTER ONE
THUNDERCHIEF

When the United States' intervention in Laos and Vietnam gathered momentum in 1965 the Republic F-105 Thunderchief was the USAF's primary fighter-bomber, having by then entered service with 24 operational squadrons and five training units. The aircraft had originally been purchased as an all-weather strike fighter, delivering tactical nuclear weapons and fighting its way past enemy interceptors on the return journey – if it survived the multiple nuclear detonations caused by many similar aircraft. For this mission it had an internal bomb-bay (unlike other contemporary fighters) and a 20 mm rotary cannon, and AIM-9B Sidewinder missiles could also be carried for self-protection.

The F-105's prolonged development delayed its initial operational service until January 1959, but by 1964 it was well established in frontline USAF nuclear alert squadrons in Europe and the Far East. Single-seat versions remained in production until January 1965.

An initial contract for 199 F-105As was awarded in September 1952 and the prototype made its first flight on 22 October 1955. The first two YF-105As flew with interim Pratt & Whitney J57-P-25 engines, but the third prototype and all subsequent F-105s had Pratt & Whitney's J75, which developed up to 26,500 lbs of thrust with afterburner and air-cooling water injection. The J75 made the aircraft the largest and most powerful single-engined fighter of its time. In combat this powerplant was the core of the F-105's success, excelling in reliability and enabling the aircraft to outdistance any rival fighter at low altitude thanks to the jet's top speed of 700+ mph. It also gave the aircraft enough muscle to haul 5000 lbs of ordnance and 900 gallons of externally-carried fuel over a 650-mile combat radius. The F-105's large fuel capacity did, however, pose limitations in combat, as a 388th Tactical Fighter Wing (TFW) pilot noted. 'You are either too heavy with fuel to be manoeuvrable or too short on fuel at fighting weight to make it back home successfully'.

Although overall weight in the final operational version (the F-105G) reached 54,600 lbs, the aircraft still used the same engine. And although the J75 developed tremendous power, the Thunderchief's acceleration from low speed in combat was comparatively slow unless the pilot nosed over into a dive. The F-105 also bled off speed very rapidly in a turn or steep climb.

Chief designer Alex Kartveli, creator of the P-47 Thunderbolt, designed a 63-ft long fuselage for the first production model, the F-105B, using semi-monocoque construction and 'area-rule' to reduce transonic drag. It contained a pressurised cockpit, gun installation, avionics, a 16-ft long weapons bay, fuel tanks and the massive engine and afterburner. Four-petal extending airbrakes were installed at the rear to slow the aircraft for weapons delivery or to enable safe aircrew ejection. The two side 'petals' extended as airbrakes for landing, although a 20-ft diameter ring-slot braking parachute provided most of the retarding force after touchdown. The F-105's fairly conventional structure used panels that were milled to the exact thickness required for optimum strength and lightness.

Wearing the yellow tail band of the Kadena-based 18th TFW, which detached Thunderchiefs from its 12th, 44th and 67th TFSs to Korat from February to October 1965, these F-105Ds carry M117 bombs (foreground) and AGM-12B Bullpup missiles for a North Vietnam strike. Seen here furthest from the camera, F-105D 62-4284 became a triple MiG killer in 1967, with two victories being credited to Capt Max Brestel and a third to Capt Gene I Basel. The nearest aircraft (62-4231) was shot down by an SA-2 on 27 October 1967 during the same mission on which Capt Basel claimed his MiG-17. One of four F-105D casualties that day, Col John Flynn, leading the mission as 388th TFW vice-commander, was rolling into his bombing dive on the Canal des Rapides Bridge when the missile struck 62-4231 (*USAF*)

The 4th TFW introduced both the F-105B and F-105D to frontline service. In August 1965 it joined the 18th and 23rd TFWs and 41st AD in deploying Thunderchiefs temporarily to Takhli and Korat, in Thailand. Many of the 4th TFW's 334th TFS F-105s had been camouflaged by then, retaining blue fin bands with white stars, but 61-0105, later the mount of MiG killer Col Bob Scott, was still silver. The limited MiG activity at that time obviated the carriage of AIM-9B missiles (*USAF*)

The wing, swept at 45 degrees, was 385 square ft in area – small for such a large airframe – and thin for high speeds. It provided stable, fast flight at low altitudes for the tactical nuclear mission in which turning performance was not a priority. However, the wing inevitably limited the F-105's ability to tackle much more manoeuvrable opposition such as the MiG-17s that it would fight over North Vietnam. As one 355th TFW pilot noted ruefully, 'air-to-air combat is still a turning game. The airplane that turns the best has the advantage'.

In order to provide clearance on rotation for the ventral fin beneath the rear fuselage the wing was mid-mounted, requiring a long, stalky undercarriage. This gave marginal clearance for a multiple ejector rack (MER) with up to six 750-lb bombs or a 450- or 650-gallon fuel tank beneath the fuselage. It also meant a long climb up to the cockpit as the canopy was more than 12 ft above the ground – the same height as the tip of a static MiG-17's tail! Two pylons could be attached below each outer wing (the undercarriage retracted inwards into the inboard wing space) and the outer pylons were usually used in combat for one or two

AN/ALQ-87 electronic countermeasures pods or an AIM-9B Sidewinder. The inboard wing sections contained engine air intakes, uniquely configured with inward-slanting lips.

Flight controls included ailerons, which operated with five-section spoilers above each wing for roll control at subsonic speeds. At higher speeds the spoilers provided all the roll control. Fowler training-edge flaps were used for takeoff and landing, and for additional lift during manoeuvring flight or, used individually, to assist with roll control. The one-piece horizontal tail was mounted low to avoid wing turbulence and the vertical fin had a rudder operated, like the other control systems, by hydraulic power from three separate systems.

For its original nuclear strike mission no protection was required for these systems, so their supply lines were run virtually parallel in the aircraft's lower fuselage. In combat this would result in many losses when hydraulic lines were hit, so another, physically separated, back-up system was added later. A Republic-designed pilot recovery system, modifying the flying controls to prevent their loss after hydraulic damage, was demonstrated at Takhli Royal Thai Air Force Base (RTAFB) in April 1967 and gradually retrofitted to all surviving F-105s.

F-105D

Weapons delivery avionics in the noses of the 75 production F-105Bs, delivered to the 4th TFW from June 1959, consisted of an MA-8 fire-control system using an E-50 sighting system (in conjunction with an E-34 radar ranging system) and an E-30 toss bombing computer. By the time the B-model entered frontline service the USAF's attention was focused on the all-weather F-105D using the R-14 North American Search and Ranging Radar System (NASARR). A 15-inch nose extension housed the R-14A radar scanner in a larger radome, replacing the E-34. Its Doppler inertial capability gave the pilot constantly updated information on his location, and it became a vital, if somewhat temperamental, navigational aid in poor visibility.

Over North Vietnam the radar was often turned off as it triggered radar-warning apparatus in other F-105s in the formation. The radar could, in

Many of the early pilots and aircraft assigned to the Vietnam War effort were transferred from the two USAFE Thunderchief wings. F-105D 60-0490, seen here in its original bare metal finish, first flew with the 36th TFW at Bitburg AB, West Germany. Unpainted aircraft were easier for the ground control approach radars to 'skin paint' if the jet's radar transponder was inoperative. Bitburg's F-105s were replaced by F-4 Phantom IIs from 1965, while the 49th TFW at Spangdahlem began to transfer its assets to Thailand at the end of 1966. This aircraft later flew with the 354th TFS/355th TFW from Takhli, bearing RM tail codes and the nickname *Captain Radio/Nuk'Em* (*USAF*)

The restricted view from the rear cockpit reduced the F-105F's effectiveness for training. Students flew their first three sorties as back-seat observers, followed by flights with the instructor flying 'chase' in another aircraft, rather than risking his well-being in the F-105F's back seat! In this F-105F the rear canopy has been blanked off by the radiation/flash shield used for nuclear weapons delivery. After service with the 36th TFW (seen here), 63-8301 was transferred to the 355th TFW. Maj Leo Thorsness and Capt Harold Johnson flew it on the Wild Weasel *mission that saw Thorsness shoot down a MiG-17, with good circumstantial evidence of a second kill, and perform the acts of bravery that resulted in him being awarded the Medal of Honor (*Author's collection*)*

theory, work with the 'guns-air' setting on the armament selection switch, but in combat many pilots found that it did not provide reliable information for the gunsight when operated below 10,000 ft (where most MiG engagements took place) due to interference from ground returns. Unless the pilot used the full radar lock-on mode the gunsight did not compensate for bullet drop over a long-distance trajectory.

In Vietnam, visual rather than radar-only identification of a potential aerial target was usually required.

Installation of the new AN/ASG-19 Thunderstick fire-control system and its avionics filled the space previously occupied by the M61A1 gun in the F-105B, resulting in the weapon being moved further back into the fuselage of the jet. D-models also had a revised cockpit layout, with some of the traditional instrument dials replaced by two vertical tape displays for quick speed and altitude reference.

The delivery of F-105Ds to the USAF commenced in March 1961 when the first examples were issued to the 4520th Combat Crew Training Wing at Nellis AFB. The first operational F-105D wing was the 36th TFW at Bitburg AB, West Germany, which received its first jets on 12 May 1961. Within four years many of its aircraft were transferred to Thailand-based combat wings for Vietnam War duties. In 1961 the USAF planned to equip 14 tactical fighter wings with the new F-105D, but President John F Kennedy's administration with its cost-cutting Defence Secretary, Robert McNamara, reduced the total to eight wings, equipping the rest with F-4 Phantom IIs. Only 610 F-105Ds were manufactured, and by 1970, when more than half had been lost in combat or accidents, a shortage of Thunderchiefs made the F-105D the only USAF aircraft to be withdrawn from frontline service because of attrition.

Two-seat F-105Fs, ordered belatedly in May 1962, replaced the last 143 F-105Ds in Republic's order book. A second cockpit was accommodated in a 31-inch fuselage extension and the area of the vertical tail was increased by 15 per cent, partly to restore the centre of gravity. Both cockpits had ejection seats, initially propelled by a ballistic pyrotechnic device but, from late 1966, they were rocket-powered. Despite limited visibility from the rear cockpit, F-105Fs were used extensively for training at Nellis AFB from mid-1966, partly because most single-seaters were already abroad in combat. Many F-models were later modified as *Wild Weasel* electronic warfare aircraft, retaining full combat capability. Three of the Thunderchief's MiG-killing encounters involved F-105Fs.

AIR-TO-AIR WEAPONS

In all operational F-105 variants a General Electric M61A1 Vulcan gun was included for strafing and self-protection. Although sometimes regarded as a secondary weapon, it was responsible for all but two of the 27.5 MiG kills credited to F-105s in the Vietnam War. The cannon was rated at 6000 rounds per minute (RPM), using hydraulic drive from the rear mounting plate. The earlier M61 variant (used as principal armament in the F-104 Starfighter) was electrically driven and limited to 4000 rpm. The M61A1's six barrels fired 20 mm M50 ammunition with 3380 ft per second muzzle velocity in bursts lasting up to 2.5 seconds. The full ammunition load, with each round weighing around one pound, was much heavier than the 275-lb gun unit itself. Shell cases and links were stored in a large cylindrical drum in the F-105D/F.

The gun was aimed via a gyroscopic, lead-computing gunsight, which was usually set for a range of 1500 ft, and a radar-ranging set. Target range (supplied by the radar) and its rate of turn (provided by the gyroscopic sight) could be combined to give acceptable accuracy. The reliability of the Vulcan cannon was generally good, considering the pressure on armourers to turn around and maintain their weapons, but the gun did fail on 10-12 per cent of firing passes – sometimes due to high g-force manoeuvres when it was fired. These failures may well have cost several additional MiG kills.

Chuck Byler, who worked on F-105 armament in the 1960s, recalled that originally the gun was 'fed by conventionally linked 20 mm ammunition, and the spent brass was dumped out the other side of the weapon. It would fire as fast as the gun could be rotated. In the F-105D model that was 1000 rpm per gun barrel or 100 rounds per second, spread over the six barrels. There was no way to change the rate of fire, nor was

Combat experience with the M61A1 dictated better gun-gas ventilation for the gun compartment through a slotted gun bay door. The utility hydraulic system receptacle was located beneath this door, in this case on 61-0105 – MiG killer Col Bob Scott's F-105D for a while when he commanded the 355th TFW (*USAF*)

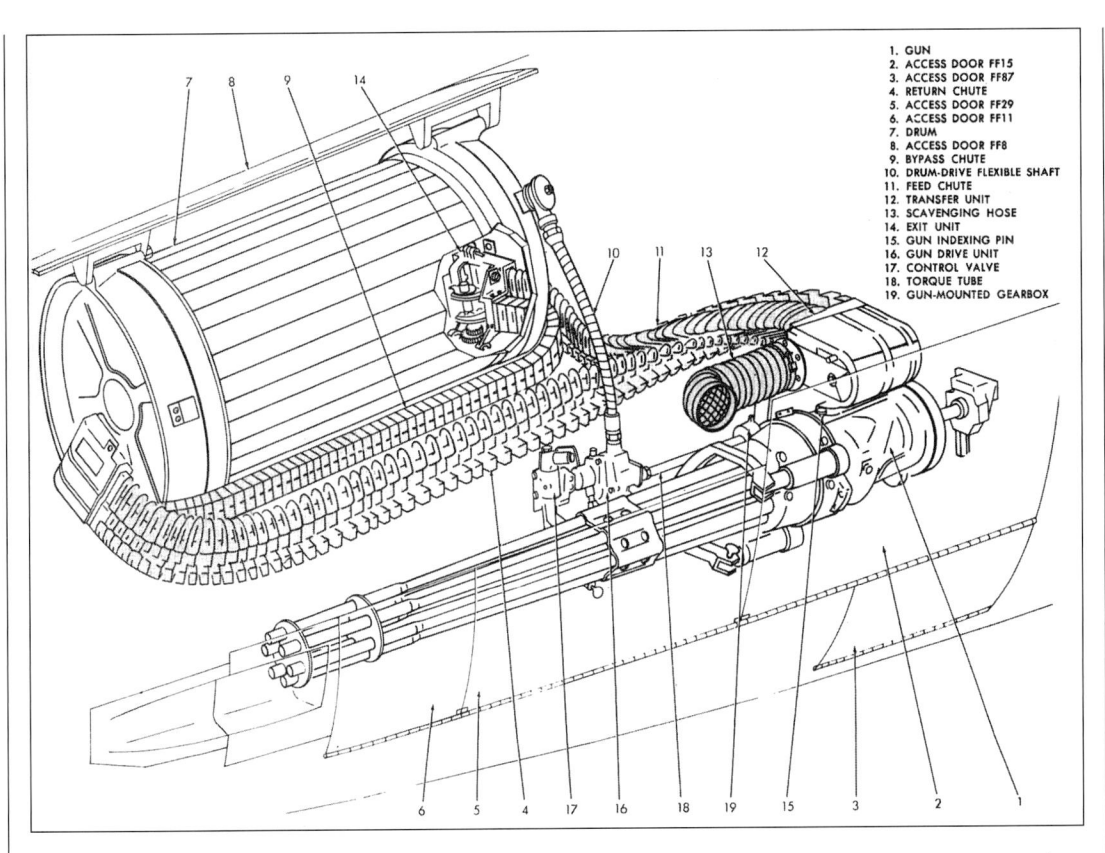

1. GUN
2. ACCESS DOOR FF15
3. ACCESS DOOR FF87
4. RETURN CHUTE
5. ACCESS DOOR FF29
6. ACCESS DOOR FF11
7. DRUM
8. ACCESS DOOR FF8
9. BYPASS CHUTE
10. DRUM-DRIVE FLEXIBLE SHAFT
11. FEED CHUTE
12. TRANSFER UNIT
13. SCAVENGING HOSE
14. EXIT UNIT
15. GUN INDEXING PIN
16. GUN DRIVE UNIT
17. CONTROL VALVE
18. TORQUE TUBE
19. GUN-MOUNTED GEARBOX

The F-105's primary weapon was the General Electric M61A1 cannon, with a supply drum holding 1028 rounds of 20 mm M50 ammunition. An evaluation board that included representatives of all the USAF tactical commands recommended reducing F-105D costs by $105,000 per aircraft by deleting the M61A1 gun, explosive suppression for the fuel tanks and ECM pod provision. Fortunately, these cuts were overruled, and all the disputed items proved absolutely vital in combat, particularly the gun. As former F-105 armament technician Chuck Byler explained, 'The standard combat load was high explosive incendiary (HEI) M50 rounds with an armour piercing incendiary (API) shell for about every seventh round. Anything short of heavy tank armour or reinforced concrete was vulnerable to this weapon' (*USAF via Chuck Byler*)

there any need to do so. Nominally, there were 1027 to 1029 rounds in the system – about ten seconds worth of ammo. A long burst would crystallise the barrels so a "burst limiter" was retro-fitted for practice purposes but eliminated for combat.

'One early problem was feeding the ammunition without breaking the traditional links that held the rounds together. The ammo was gobbled up so fast that the links often broke. In the F-105D/F the linkless feed system recycled spent rounds back into the drum, which was initially loaded on the ground and then hoisted into the bay. Once installed, the drum was re-loaded in place in the aircraft nose. A McCullough chainsaw engine was adapted to use shaft drive, which propelled a transfer unit mounted on top of the gun. During the re-loading process conventionally linked ammo was de-linked by the transfer unit and fed, one round at a time, into the six sliding bolts of the gun. The bolts had a roller that ran in an elliptical cam path in and out of the barrel chambers.

'Conveyor belt units fed the live ammunition into the gun and then back to the other side of the drum. Those belts had what looked like conventional links in them, but they did not grip the rounds the way a conventional link does. The outside of the ammunition drum was a series of slats bolted together, with the grooved side of the slats facing the interior of the drum. The live ammunition, and spent rounds, slid along in those grooves, driven by a giant heli-coil, with the shells held in the slats by the extractor groove at the base of each round so that the bullets pointed towards the interior of the drum. One missing round would cause a jam because the rounds would tip and bind in the track formed by the slats. The gun itself rarely malfunctioned or jammed. Jams most often occurred in the drum or on the conveyor belts in the feed system.

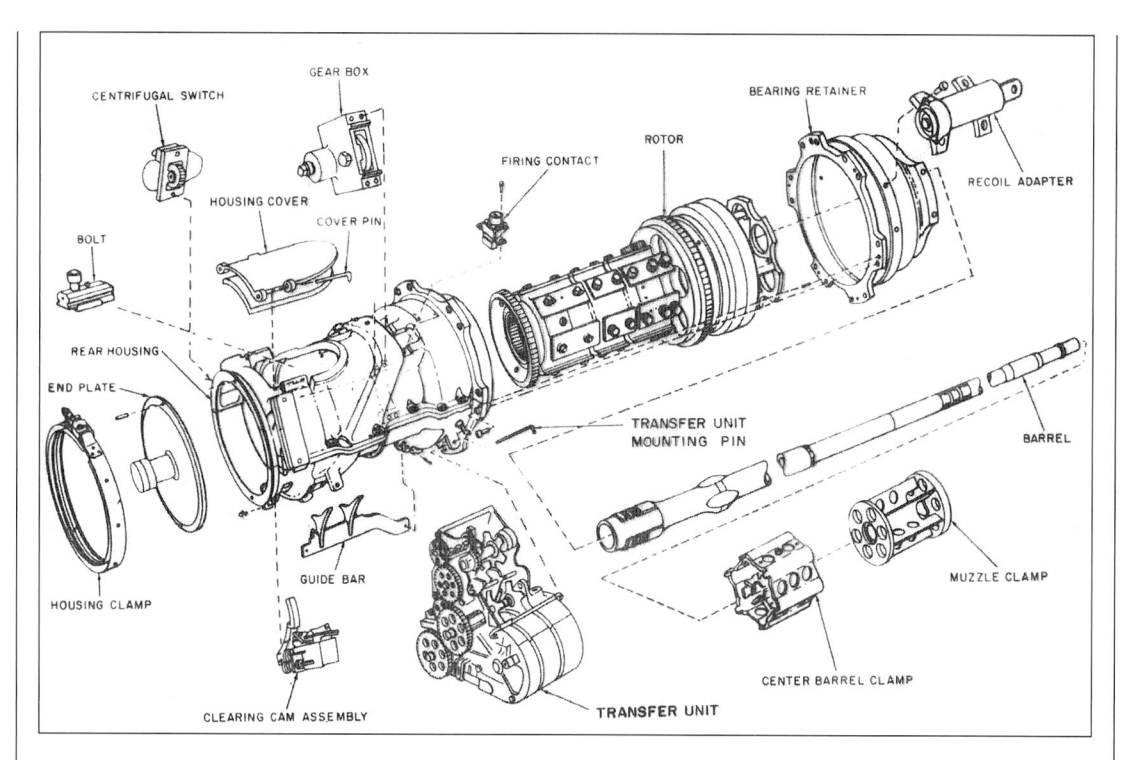

'We were supposed to change the barrels after six re-loadings of the system. When I first arrived at Bitburg AB in 1963 there had been no maintenance to speak of on the guns because no-one had been through technical school training to learn how. Repairs were done on an emergency basis. My first job was stripping down, cleaning and rebuilding these "Gatling" guns, some of which had sand in them from the practice range in Libya. Usually, I had to replace all six bolts and the track they slid in. Often, I replaced every part of the gun, including the housing, except for the rotor, which was considered the equivalent of a "receiver" in a conventional rifle or hand-gun. I found one gun with a rotor so chewed up that the gun had to be scrapped. It was still firing despite all the damage.

'The simple beauty of the Vulcan gun design was that it rotated like a turbine rather than chugging back and forth like other machine guns. Jim Kasler [a famous Vietnam F-105 pilot] never had a gun malfunction or jam during his 91 combat missions, and he fired the weapon at secondary targets whenever the opportunity arose. Apparently none of the mission planners [in Vietnam] thought of the gun as a primary weapon, but many of Kasler's targets were destroyed with it.'

Although it was only used successfully in three of the Thunderchief's MiG kills, the Ford Aerospace/Raytheon AIM-9B Sidewinder infrared homing missile was carried on most F-105 missions over North Vietnam from December 1966 onwards. The weapon originated at the US Navy's China Lake Naval Ordnance Test Station as a one-man venture by engineer William B McLean. His simple design used an aluminium tube, nine moving parts, a rocket motor and a heat-seeking cell. Its first successful test took place on 11 September 1953, and in comparative tests with the

Despite the impression given by this exploded view, the M61A1 was a relatively simple, reliable weapon. Its gunsight and fire-control systems presented more problems than the weapon itself, and many of the F-105's MiG kills were achieved by cruder methods such as using the pitot boom on the aircraft's nose as a rudimentary gunsight. The complexity of the armament system's 'switchology' could catch out even the most experienced pilots, and probably accounted for numerous instances of accidentally jettisoned bombs, tanks and pylons, as well as missiles that were fired at the wrong moment (*USAF via Chuck Byler*)

USAF's much more complex and expensive Hughes AIM-4 Falcon it proved to be more reliable. Production began in 1956, and the AIM-9 soon became the world's most successful and widely used air-to-air missile.

The AIM-9B, the first of many production variants, was used by all three United States services throughout Operation *Rolling Thunder*. It was selected for the F-105 during the earliest design discussions in December 1954. Measuring 111.4 inches, with fins spanning 15 inches, the missile had a 12.5-lb Mk 8 blast-fragmentation warhead detonated by a Mk 304 influence fuse. An un-cooled lead-sulphide infrared seeker head was installed on its nose, covered by a glass dome that was susceptible to scratching or blurring by heat friction in high-Mach low-altitude flight. Indeed, the missile itself sometimes became scorched and damaged by high-speed friction.

Early AIM-9s had to be fired from almost directly behind a non-manoeuvring target emitting a strong heat signature to home successfully, and they could be distracted by the sun, ground heat, clouds or by being launched outside the tight range parameters required. Minimum range was 3000 ft (more if the launch aircraft was travelling much faster than its target) and the maximum range was around 3500 ft. Ideally, it was launched at a target with a clear sky background but not within 15 degrees of the sun. Careful judgement was required to comply with those distances, and even then the missile would fail to guide if either the launch aircraft or its target entered a turn of more than 2gs. F-105 pilots sometimes found that when they selected the missile to test its infrared seeker acquisition tone the missile would just fire off un-commanded.

A twin-Sidewinder launcher was devised to attach below the F-105's outer pylons, but this was considered too drag-inducing in combat and it could not be jettisoned. A low-drag single 'Slim Jim' launcher was introduced in late 1966 as a 355th TFW field-modification. Some pilots resented losing pylon ordnance space to the missiles and others felt that their drag outweighed their usefulness. Missile performance was reduced at lower altitudes by increased drag and ground heat, and the AIM-9B never achieved the 65 per cent success rate predicted by tests that were usually conducted in the most favourable conditions for the missile.

Single AIM-9Bs were often hung only on the flight and element leaders' aircraft from December 1966, and were seldom loaded for missions into the lower MiG-threat areas. This was partly because of supply problems, as legendary F-105 pilot Col Jack Broughton explained;

Armourers carry out the daily routine of loading the F-105s with replenished ammunition drums and removing spent rounds, using an F-2A or MHU-12A/M trailer with a large ammunition box (seen above the last letters of *EXPLOSIVE A*). The armourer nearest the cockpit is operating the powered loader. Spent material was deposited from a chute into the open container (left) (*USAF*)

'We were always short of Sidewinders, thus the number carried depended on how many we had at engine start time. If we had them we loaded them. They were always nice to have in case you got on a MiG and had time to set the switches up to get the missile ready to fire.'

On the few occasions when F-105 pilots had a chance to use the AIM-9B effectively, the missile showed that even the early versions of the Sidewinder could bring down a MiG with a single hit or very near miss. Of the 11 missiles fired from F-105s between 23 April and 8 July 1967 three scored hits, compared with 12 out of 21 Vulcan gun attacks that hit or probably hit their targets. However, pilots felt that several more MiG kills could have occurred if their F-105s had been carrying Sidewinders. The more effective AIM-9E model entered service in 1969, and it performed well during the Operation *Linebacker I/II* campaigns of 1972, although F-105D/Fs had by then stopped bombing in areas where MiGs might be encountered.

THE OPPOSITION

Although F-105 crews were engaged by supersonic MiG-21s over North Vietnam, and they caused 15 Thunderchief losses (principally with their primary armament of two AA-2A (K-13) 'Atoll' missiles, which were essentially AIM-9B copies) without suffering a single casualty in return, the majority of engagements – nine-tenths of F-105 firing opportunities and all of their aerial kills – involved the MiG-17. A development of the MiG-15 (which some senior Thunderchief pilots had fought in the skies above North Korea in the early 1950s), the MiG-17 was much smaller and more agile than the F-105 as it had been designed for aerial combat, with a secondary attack capability – the exact opposite of the Thunderchief.

Col Robin Olds, commanding the Phantom II-equipped 8th TFW that provided much of the escort protection for F-105 strikes, observed;

'That little airplane can give you a tussle the likes of which you have never had before in your life. It's fast enough. It turns on a dime. It has a reasonable zoom capability. It has a very light wing loading. I've seen them "Split-S" from 2000 ft. It's absolutely impossible to follow them. I've seen the MiG quickly turn from where I had him at a disadvantage – perhaps 30 degrees angle off about a mile-and-a-half out and trying to get a missile shot at him – to him being in a position to make a firing pass at me when I was doing Mach 0.9 and closing. The jet's turn radius has to be seen to be believed. It's incredible.'

The MiG-17 entered Soviet service in 1953, five years before the F-105B, and almost 11,000 were built at five factories in the USSR. Examples were also constructed in China as the Shenyang J-5. The Vietnamese People's Air Force (VPAF, or Khong Quan Vham Dan Viet Nam) received MiGs and training from both nations. A small afterburner was added to the fighter's Klimov VF-1F turbojet engine (a cloned Rolls-Royce Nene), which doubled the fighter's climb performance but only added 30 mph to its top speed. The afterburner took more than five seconds to ignite, and it had to be shut off after three minutes at altitudes below 23,000 ft, where most combat engagements occurred. This restriction duly limited the MiG's ability to catch or escape from enemy fighters. Basic engine acceleration was slow, taking around 15 seconds from idle to maximum power. A few of the earliest VPAF examples were MiG-17 'Fresco-A' models without afterburners.

The engines in both the MiG-17 and MiG-21 had the great advantage of leaving only slight smoke-trails (unlike American turbojets), making them hard to see at a distance, particularly head-on.

In the F-105, engaging afterburner increased engine thrust from 16,100 lbs to 24,500 lbs – more than four times the MiG-17's full power output. The MiG-17F could achieve 650 mph at 36,000 ft compared with the F-105D's 1192 mph at the same altitude. The VPAF jet was limited to Mach 1.25 in a steep dive. Indeed, it tended to pull itself out of the dive at that speed. At high subsonic speeds and lower altitude (below 15,000 ft) the MiG's mechanically-operated flying controls felt so heavy – despite a lengthened control column for more leverage – that manoeuvring was almost impossible, even with hydraulically power-boosted ailerons. Aerodynamic loads on the un-powered tail control surfaces made control forces of more than 2g difficult to 'pull' at high speeds, and pilots often had to use both hands on the control column to roll. However, at 300 to 350 knots a 7g turn was perfectly feasible.

At low-altitude speeds above 400 knots MiG-17s lost longitudinal stability and tended to roll. Severe buffeting in that situation, particularly when turning, prevented the pilot from using his gunsight effectively due to vibration. Pilots therefore tried to restrict dogfights to lower speeds, where they had the advantage. External ordnance loads were limited to two 550-lb bombs or two drag-inducing 88-gallon drop tanks.

A slow-reacting afterburner and heavy control forces were also weaknesses in early MiG-21s. However, the MiG-21 accelerated faster than an F-105, and if the VPAF pilot was within 'Atoll' range and the Thunderchief used afterburner to escape, the heat-seeking missile had an ideal target. The F-105 pilot's best defensive tactic against a MiG-21 was to turn in towards it and dive away, or he could extend his air-brakes, forcing the MiG to overshoot. His maximum low-altitude speed of around 730 knots (compared with 595 knots for the MiG-21) was also a clear advantage, but North Vietnamese ground-controlled

A camouflaged MiG-17F shares the ramp with MiG-21PFMs and earlier MiG-21F-13s. MiGs could strike at any stage during a mission, but favourite ambush spots on the F-105s' predictable routes were around a turn point (Channel 97), over the valley near Hoa Binh that contained the Route 12 highway and along 'Phantom Ridge', a mountainous chain north of Haiphong. Most MiGs in 1966-67 were located at Phuc Yen, Kep and Gia Lam (Hanoi Airport), but Cat Bi, Kien An (near Haiphong) and Hoa Lac were also used. MiGs could remain airborne in target areas for 50 minutes. At Yen Bai they were dispersed via roads to holding areas up to four miles from the bases, or kept in caves holding up to 20 aircraft – here, they were maintained by Soviet and Vietnamese technicians. MiGs were responsible for only 23 of the 397 F-105 losses suffered by the USAF in the Vietnam conflict (*via Dr István Toperczer*)

interception (GCI) operators soon became adept at positioning MiG-21s behind F-105s in their 'blind spot'.

The USAF's Project *Feather Duster*, which developed air-to-air fighter tactics, included test engagements in August 1966 between F-105s and F-86H Sabres (simulating MiG-17s and MiG-19s). These showed that the F-105 would usually lose if it entered low-speed manoeuvring with the Sabre. An F-105 pilot's best move was a high-speed escape at low altitude, 'jinking' and feinting turns to throw off the attacker's gun tracking and remaining close to the ground to prevent missiles from attaining a clear radar target.

If the F-105 pilots chose to engage, their best tactic was the 'double attack' promoted by Col John Boyd, in which two F-105s used their speed advantage to conduct individual attacks on a MiG from different angles. However, this proposal contravened established USAF doctrine of maintaining the integrity of four-aircraft 'fighting wing' flights in which the flight leader was the main 'shooter', supported by the other three flight members. The latter had to keep formation with him throughout his attempts to engage an enemy, and they only had firing opportunities if the leader allowed them. Ten of the F-105's MiG kills were made by flight leader pilots, nine by leaders of the second element and only two by 'No 4' men in the flight.

In high-speed flight at low altitude the F-105's powered controls (with stability augmentation) and its relatively small, thin wing made flight smooth and stable. Like the MiG-21, the MiG-17 was built for strong Soviet pilots rather than their smaller and lighter VPAF counterparts, who in turn had problems with the fighter's heavy controls and its instability in yawing movements that made accurate gunnery difficult. However, over North Vietnam, the technical performance advantages of US aircraft flying strike missions were compromised by the weight and drag of their external ordnance and the need to preserve rigid defensive formations. These restrictions usually handed the initiative to the MiG pilots when the USAF and VPAF clashed.

The MiG-17's strengths were its light weight, exceptional manoeuvrability at lower speeds and its heavy cannon 'artillery'. The wing, swept at 45 degrees, was increased to 243 sq ft in area compared to the MiG-15's 221.5 sq ft, while the fuselage was lengthened by 2 ft 11 ins to 36 ft 4 ins. With an overall maximum weight of 13,267 lbs, including drop tanks, the MiG-17F 'Fresco-C' weighed around a quarter of the F-105D's 52,838 lbs maximum takeoff weight. Lower wing-loading and the MiG's shorter fuselage in relation to its wingspan enabled Vietnamese pilots to disengage combat at will, or make a snap roll which could easily be converted into a turn, placing the MiG behind a Thunderchief in seconds and ready to open fire if the USAF pilot did not engage afterburner to accelerate and outdistance it. This MiG-17 turn was equally effective against F-4 Phantom IIs and even F-14A Tomcats and F-16A Fighting Falcons in secret trials staged in the US in the 1970s.

Using Soviet doctrine, pilots were trained to attack from the rear or head-on, with the more difficult possibility of approaches at right angles, turning in behind the potential victim if the MiG's speed greatly exceeded the target aircraft's at the time. However, their best option was to try and break up F-105 flights, disorientate the pilots and then attack those who failed to regain their positions. Maj Dale W Lathem, the 355th TFW's standards and evaluation officer in 1967, asserted that several F-105s were lost in this way. 'When the flight was together and the force was together there was quite a hesitancy for them to attack. They would rather sit off and pick off the stragglers'. The tactic worked equally well for F-105 pilots, with several MiGs being shot down after losing the protection of their other flight members.

Use of afterburner to get out of trouble rapidly exhausted the F-105's fuel reserves, requiring the pilot to withdraw to a safe area and a tanker aircraft. MiG pilots had no aerial refuelling capability, but they were usually operating close to their bases in any case. However, the MiG-17's internal fuel capacity of only 374 gallons (less fuel than was held in one F-105 drop tank!) limited its combat endurance. Indeed, many MiGs were lost through fuel starvation.

GUN FOR GUN

Compared with the F-105's 'chainsaw' M61A1, the armament fitted to the MiG-17 was from an earlier era, its single Nudel'man N-37D 37mm cannon having originated during World War 2. When the pilot squeezed the red gun button lever on his control column, the weapon fired 26.5 ounce shells at 400 rpm, and a single hit in a vulnerable area could cripple an aircraft. American pilots said they could clearly see individual shells emerging like orange fireballs from the gun, accompanied by a long red flame for each round. Only 40 rounds were carried, but the aircraft also had two Nudel'man-Rikhter NR-23 23 mm cannon in its nose, each able to fire 650 rpm, with 80 rounds per gun. The MiG-17's combined weight of fire was therefore considerable – more than 35 lbs of projectiles per second, for six seconds, effective at ranges of more than 3500 ft, but with only half the F-105's firing time and aimed with a primitive gunsight.

VPAF armourers replenish the 37 mm N-37D (foreground) and two 23 mm NR-23 guns of a MiG-17, which have been accessed by winching down the guns and their ammunition boxes. In February 1967 US intelligence agencies estimated that the VPAF had 73 MiG-17s and 18 MiG-21s on strength, falling to 41 and 15, respectively, by June of that year (*via Dr István Toperczer*)

MiG-17s had tough, simple airframes that were easy to maintain without the complex, vulnerable systems and electronics of their American counterparts. Pilots, however, had poor visibility over the high canopy side-rails and bulbous fuselage sides. The frame of the bubble canopy and the ejection seat blocked off most of the rear view, requiring an external periscope. Their forward view was degraded by a thick windshield and frame and by the bulky ASP-4NM gunsight unit. The ejection seat could only be adjusted in height with seat pads, tailored to each pilot. Visibility from the MiG-21 cockpit, particularly the later versions, was also poor, and American pilots took advantage of that.

F-105 pilots attempted to direct the focused stream of 20 mm shells from their guns at a MiG-17's weaker points – the engine, cockpit and the 36-gallon fuel tank in the rear fuselage beneath the jet tailpipe. Because the Vulcan's concentrated bullet stream made it a 'no hits or 100 per cent hits' weapon, F-105 pilots often tended to 'stir the stick' (control column) to disperse the shells and increase the chances of a hit. If the entire stream could be directed at the target the Vulcan could cut off a wing or tail. The gunsight 'pipper' (aiming circle) was usually placed well ahead of a turning MiG so that it would fly into the bullets from the F-105, which would be turning less tightly.

Both fighters presented their pilots with difficulties when it came to sighting their weapons effectively. A MiG pilot was hampered by vibration, an inadequate gunsight that 'lost' its aim point if the pilot was following an adversary in a turn, poor gun harmonisation and the aircraft's lack of stability at high speeds, which caused shells to scatter in the air. The best bet was to get in as close as possible to the target aircraft before firing – for F-105 pilots their training suggested a minimum of 1000 ft behind the target, with a functioning gunsight and radar tracking.

The F-105 was a much more stable gun platform but its pilot had to perform a complex series of switch changes to re-set his weapons controls and gunsight to air-to-air (gun or missile) rather than its ground-attack mode, since the same sight mechanism was

A typical F-105D cockpit. The radar control panel is below the radar display screen at the base of the main panel. Below that is the weapons control panel, with a relatively inaccessible weapons circuit breaker panel at floor level. The cockpit was large and well appointed, although in combat some pilots found that the canopy structure exaggerated glare and internal reflection problems, particularly if it was scratched. An ashtray was provided for smokers, who were made aware of the dangers of lighting up with oxygen flowing from their facemasks – a few sustained burns despite this (*Gary Chambers*)

used for both purposes. The five requisite switches were small and situated low in the cockpit, requiring the pilot to take his eyes off the target for several seconds, during which time a firing opportunity might well be lost. Pilots who had flown the F-86 Sabre and F-100 Super Sabre preferred their quicker, simpler switching procedures.

Ten of the F-105's MiG kills were made without the gunsight when there was no time to adjust it properly and the pilot merely sighted along the nose of his aircraft, sometimes using the nose pitot probe as a primitive aiming device. Ten kills were made in around 40 gun attacks where the pilot had the use of a gunsight. *Iron Hand* flights armed with cluster bomb units to attack SAM and AAA sites could often keep their gunsights set for air-to-air since the delivery of cluster bombs did not require the same accuracy as 'iron' bombs.

The 'heads down' switch-setting problem was exacerbated by restricted vision from the cockpit, particularly to the rear, and by the need to maintain a relatively tight 'fighting wing' combat formation in which aircraft had to stay in set positions about 500 to 1000 ft apart, demanding constant visual reference to the rest of the flight. Making sure that the flight was not being pursued by MiGs required manoeuvring to see behind and below the aircraft, and tight formations made this difficult.

Fighting the MiG-17 and MiG-21 over North Vietnam provided American pilots with their only realistic understanding of the two fighters' capabilities before 1968, when Israel loaned the USA a MiG-21F-13, delivered by an Iraqi defector in 1966. It was tested at Groom Lake (Area 51) in Project *Have Doughnut*. MiG-17s were not accessible until 1969 when Israel again provided Syrian examples that had become lost during an exercise. They too were tested in Projects *Have Drill* and *Have Ferry*, and one MiG-17 was retained at Groom Lake, where it was joined by other acquired MiGs from 1972.

THE ROAD TO WAR

Compared with the USAF, the VPAF's history was a short one. Until 1956 it had a handful of aged French and British aircraft, but in March of that year 110 student pilots were sent to China for basic training, while others went to the Krasnodar Flight Officers' School in the USSR and to Czechoslovakia for instruction. In 1960 the first batch of 52 pilots began conversion training on the MiG-17 at Mong Tu, in China, near the North Vietnamese border. Trained pilots began to return to North Vietnam at the end of 1962, and in February 1964 the Soviet Union donated 36 MiG-17s and two-seat MiG-15UTIs (both long obsolete as interceptors in the USSR) to form the first VPAF fighter squadron, the 921st 'Sao Do' Fighter Regiment (FR) at Phuc Yen (Noi Bai) airfield. It was fully operational by August 1964 when US air attacks began in the wake of the Gulf of Tonkin incident.

The Soviet *Journal of Military Thought* mentioned the 'extremely acute problem of training Vietnamese personnel to use modern weapons competently', and that the 'first and most important step in increasing the effectiveness of the [North Vietnamese] air defence was the establishment of a radar field [early warning system]'. It also noted that 'the air defence system by the end of 1965 still remained inadequately organised', and that the North Vietnamese were reluctant to follow the Soviet doctrine of concentrating air defences around the country's 'most important installations', preferring instead a kind of 'guerrilla ambush approach' throughout the country. The report considered that poor coordination of defence assets and inadequate use of early warning equipment continued throughout 1966.

Thirty more pilots returned from training in the USSR in the summer of 1965, allowing the formation of a second MiG-17 unit, the 923rd 'Yen The' FR. MiG-21 pilots began training with the 921st FR from January 1966. From March 1964, when the 921st FR was first put on full alert, until the MiG-21's combat debut on 23 April 1966, the VPAF's aerial opposition to US air activities was exclusively the responsibility of MiG-17 pilots and their 36 aircraft. There was much debate during the war over the possibility that Soviet pilots were flying some of the VPAF's combat missions, as they had done for the North Koreans during the Korean War, but the North Vietnamese and Russians still assert today that their only flying activity was for training purposes as 'advisors', not actual combat.

The crews who manned the F-105s of the 6441st TFW (the first unit to deploy aircraft to Korat RTAFB, in Thailand, in August 1964) flying from Yokota AB, Japan, were often senior officers, many with fighter experience during the Korean War and/or World War 2. Korat hosted temporary deployments (TDY) by elements of the 18th TFW later in 1964, and they began *Barrel Roll* armed reconnaissance missions against infiltration routes in Laos at the end of that year.

As the demand for F-105 missions increased, the 355th TFW was sent to a second Thai air base at Takhli on permanent change of station (PCS) status in November 1965, having already rotated some of its squadrons to the base earlier in the year, together with units from the Kansas-based 23rd TFW. In March 1966 Korat RTAFB, 155 miles east of Takhli, became home for the 388th TFW, reactivated on 14 March 1966 (PCS) with two F-105 squadrons and adding two more in May 1966.

Many of the F-105 pilots involved in these deployments were already well versed in aerial combat, as former 355th TFW vice wing commander and Korean War veteran Col Jacksel Broughton told the author;

'Most of us old heads in the "Thud" business had a good grasp on aerial combat. I don't think air-to-air was ever considered irrelevant in training, at least not at our level. We didn't have very many trainees join us during my time in Southeast Asia. We needed experienced guys to go North, and if we got a new guy we taught him all we could on-scene.'

As Col Robin Olds remarked, 'Unfortunately, you can't train a man in the United States for what he has to do in combat'. That level of realistic training was not approached until Nellis AFB began *Red Flag* exercises in November 1975.

For MiG-17 pilots their introduction to air combat was a much more tentative business. Their Soviet and Chinese mentors showed them the rudiments of simple 'dogfighting' and ground attack in fair weather, but they usually fired live ammunition only six or eight times before commencing combat duties. Training concentrated on complying with the rigid Soviet-equipped radar warning and ground control structure of the Air Defence Forces (ADF-VPAF), which guided pilots to their targets,

Maj William J Kriz (44th TFS) with a reminder of the F-105's main purpose over North Vietnam. A clutch of six 750-lb M117A Tritonal-filled demolition bombs was the usual load for most targets. Ground clearance for the lowest bomb was a mere seven inches. En route to his aircraft a pilot carried almost his own weight in gear, including his helmet (costing $500) in a bag and another 'brain bag' full of charts, checklists, target photos and navigation data. His parachute weighed 50 lbs, a g-suit covered his body from the waist down and his survival vest held a flashlight, fishing kit, water, gun, ammunition, two knives and radios, a saw and a first aid kit. For MiG killer Maj 'Mo' Seaver, who ejected from F-105s twice, the RT-10 survival radio was 'the most essential item for my recovery' (*Maj William Kriz*)

cleared them to fire and then arranged their escape from US fighters escorting a strike force. This Soviet model of fighter control, using P-35 and PRV-11 warning radars, usually required pilots to stay out of areas where AAA or SAM batteries had freedom to fire (although several MiGs were hit by 'friendly fire'). However, it placed them in the best positions for making attacking passes on F-105 formations and then diving for home before the American fighters could react.

The USAF's airborne radar controllers were less able to detect and monitor the MiG elements from their offshore radar patrol stations, particularly when MiGs attacked from low altitudes.

F-105 pilots generally had had much more thorough training, although most of this was in strike tactics with nuclear or conventional ordnance. Many of the early contingents of pilots, and their aircraft, at the Thai bases came from USAFE units in West Germany, where they were used to unfavourable weather conditions – good preparation for the rain, cloud and poor visibility that blighted Southeast Asia for much of the year. Their regular visits to the ranges near Wheelus AB in Libya provided practice in air-to-ground weapons delivery, including strafing with the Vulcan gun. However, comparatively little time was devoted to air-to-air tactics. After two years of combat flying against VPAF fighters many pilots wondered why they had never received dissimilar air combat training against manoeuvrable MiG-simulator aircraft such as the F-86H Sabre and F-102A Delta Dagger, rather than a few mock engagements with other F-105s.

Strike training focused on missions involving single jets rather than the large formations of four-aircraft flights that would be standard for

Operation *Rolling Thunder* missions over North Vietnam from 2 March 1965. In these wartime strike packages F-105 pilots were required to maintain formation in the Korean War-vintage 'Fluid Four' flights (still taught at the USAF's Fighter Weapons School course on advanced air-to-air tactics throughout the time that F-105 pilots were combating MiGs) in which three of the pilots spent much of their time just keeping formation with the flight leader. They had to push through the unprecedentedly multi-layered defences with heavy bomb-loads that severely restricted their manoeuvrability, make their individual bombing runs and re-formate off target to offer mutual protection on the exit journey. Fully loaded F-105s struggled to climb above 18,000 ft, allowing MiG-21 attacks from above. They were restricted to predictable routes, times and radio call-signs, making the VPAF defenders' task easier.

Initially, it was assumed that F-105s would not require fighter escorts, as the fledgling VPAF was not considered a threat. There was little change in USAF air-to-air training until after 1972.

COMBAT BEGINS

With widely differing preparation for war and aircraft that had little in common, the MiG-17 and F-105 pilots clashed for the first time on 4 April 1965 – the day after the 921st FR had made its combat debut. A US Navy strike on bridges in Than Hoa province on 3 April was met by four Phuc Yen-based MiG-17s, which engaged F-8E Crusaders and damaged one with gunfire. Their effect on the force of 48 F-105s attacking the Ham Rong ('Dragon's Jaw') bridge the following day was far more severe.

'Zinc' flight of 354th TFS F-105Ds was forced to orbit at 325 knots with heavy bomb loads of eight 750-lb M117s, plus two 450-gallon drop tanks, ten miles south of their bridge target because of timing problems with the tanker force. Noticing their vulnerable position, ADF-VPAF ground controllers vectored a flight of MiG-17s into a stern attack from

Camouflage was introduced in mid-1965 to replace the F-105's earlier Project *Look Alike* silver acrylic lacquer protective finish. USAFE and PACAF F-105D/Fs received the Basic Tactical Scheme using around 20 gallons of acrylic nitro-cellulose. This aircraft (60-0505), armed with BLU-1 napalm canisters but still without 'dog-ear' rear fuselage air intakes, has an early style of serial presentation and the national insignia low on the fuselage. 60-0505 (later nicknamed *25 Ton Canary* and *Fighting Irishman*) fought with both Thailand-based wings, surviving until 18 February 1969 when its tail was shot off by AAA during a bombing run over Laos. Capt John Brucher ejected safely but he was captured and never returned – the fate of many US airmen who were shot down over that country (*USAF*)

high altitude. There was no airborne radar protection for US strike formations at this stage of the war and pilots had to rely on their own alertness to spot enemy fighters. MiGs had been sighted the previous day but they had not engaged the strike force.

'Zinc 3' (Maj Vernon M Kulla) and '4' (Capt Richard P Pearson) saw the four MiGs emerging from the haze and called several warnings to their flight leader. 'Zinc 1' (Maj Frank Bennett) and his wingman apparently did not hear the calls (probably because the airwaves were jammed with other transmissions from more than 80 US aircraft in the area) and continued to orbit, while 'Zinc 3', flown by an experienced, but unnamed, ex-F-100 Super Sabre pilot, jettisoned his bombs and set up his Vulcan gun for an engagement. 'Zinc 4', an F-105 gunnery instructor, was unable to complete the complex weapons set-up sequence in time and he lost sight of the MiGs.

In the hit and run engagement that followed the MiG flight leader, Tran Hanh, hit F-105D 59-1754 with all three guns from a range of 1500 ft. The badly damaged Thunderchief headed out to sea, losing hydraulic pressure. Bennett eventually ejected just short of Da Nang AB when his oil pressure reached zero, but he drowned because his parachute did not open fully. The remaining three F-105 pilots turned to engage the MiGs, but 'Zinc 2' (59-1764) was immediately hit by gunfire from Le Minh Huan's light grey MiG-17 and it crashed into the sea, killing Capt James Magnusson.

'Zinc 3' was also attacked and damaged by two MiGs, and he evaded them by performing a snap roll, thereby slowing to make them overshoot. It was a tactic he recalled from his instructor at the Tactical Weapons Center, the legendary Capt John R Boyd. At the time he had dismissed the idea, but on 4 April it put a MiG-17 right in his gunsight, although he was so surprised that he missed the opportunity of a kill. He pushed the power up to maximum, descending to 500 ft to recover from his manoeuvre.

One MiG was seen diving vertically close to the ground, and it may have crashed. A third F-105D from another flight was downed by AAA over the target, but three VPAF fighters failed to return that day. The pilot of one MiG-17 may have lost control and crashed during the engagement, while the others were possibly hit by friendly fire as they returned to Phuc Yen. One of the latter aircraft was the MiG flown by Le Minh Huan, who died in the resulting crash. Tran Hanh, the only pilot in the MiG flight to survive after crash-landing his MiG, stated that all three jets had been shot down by F-105s, but no claims were made by pilots from the 355th TFW. One MiG-17 may well have been shot down by Capt Don Kilgus from the 416th TFS F-100D Super Sabre CAP flight in another part of the target area.

In their opening engagement with F-105s the MiG pilots had destroyed the first two US aircraft to be lost in aerial combat during the war. Their loss caused surprise and concern in the Pentagon, where a 'primitive' and 'obsolete' fighter like the MiG-17 had not been considered a real threat to America's technological superiority. It would be 15 months before the F-105 force began to restore the balance. During that time 90 more F-105s were lost in Southeast Asia, although only one of these fell to a MiG pilot.

CHAPTER TWO

'THUDS' FIGHT BACK

Thunderchief crews downed roughly one-fifth of the 135 MiGs destroyed by USAF fighters during the Vietnam War. The others fell to F-4 Phantom IIs. However, those F-105 MiG kills were scored within about 18 months between 29 June 1966 (when the threat from MiGs became more consistent) and 19 December 1967. Phantom II crews accumulated their kills between 10 July 1965 and 7 January 1973, a period about five times longer, although during the four-year 'bombing pause' from late 1968 through to the spring of 1972 USAF aircraft seldom encountered MiGs.

At some points in the F-105's months of MiG battles their rate of aerial victories rivalled that of the F-4, and they had more engagements with MiGs than any other US aircraft. This was all the more remarkable since the F-105s were invariably involved in bombing missions while the MiG-killing Phantom II crews were mostly assigned to combat air patrol (CAP) or escort missions, where their primary role was to fend off MiGs and protect the strike force F-105s. As MiG-killer G I Basel observed, 'An enemy plane destroyed was not a usual thing for us. We [F-105s] were bombers – we knocked down bridges and avoided the enemy fighters if we could'.

Also, F-4s were configured with up to eight air-to-air missiles (compared with one or two on some F-105s), and in the case of the F-4E Phantom II the same internal gun as the F-105 or, for F-4C and F-4D variants, external gun pods that were used in ten kills.

Hunting MiGs was not on the F-105 pilots' agenda, and their kills usually arose from defensive responses during bombing missions. The 388th TFW Operations Instructions prescribed the following procedures in the event of a MiG attack;

'The escort flight of F-4s will first deploy to engage the attacking MiGs. Once the escort flight has engaged or has been separated for any reason the strike force will assume its own escort responsibility. This may be accomplished in two ways. The strike force may move in a diamond formation, with No 4 flight [the final flight] assuming escort responsibilities. This F-105 escort flight still has the primary responsibility of bombing the target, but it is authorised to jettison ordnance and then engage for the purpose of aiding the rest of the force to hit the target. The escort first makes a shallow turn and then jettisons ordnance and engages if the MiGs have not yet been deterred. The second option keeps the force in the "box" [formation], with the two rearmost flights becoming the escorts. The flight on the side of the attack goes through the same procedure as the No 4 flight in the diamond formation.'

A MiG pilot's principal objective was to make F-105s jettison their ordnance and lose formation integrity. On several occasions this caused near-collisions between F-105 flights as they dispersed, sometimes leaving stray flight members for MiGs to focus upon. Exposure to enemy defences occupied a relatively small part of each mission, as MiG killer Lt Col Arthur Dennis observed. 'An average mission takes about 3.5 hours of flying, with from five to fifteen minutes over the target. The dive-bomb run is when the aircraft is most vulnerable to enemy ground fire, but there isn't much time to worry about it – there's too many things to be done' (*USAF*)

During those 18 months of Thunderchief versus MiG engagements the F-4 squadrons shot down 21 MiG-17s, compared with 27.5 by F-105 pilots. One kill was shared with a Phantom II crew. The remaining 21 enemy fighters destroyed by Phantom IIs during that period were MiG-21s. These much faster, missile-firing interceptors tended to make supersonic, one-pass attacks from behind the US strike formations, escaping at high speed and seldom putting themselves within range of the Thunderchiefs' guns. They often left the F-105s for MiG-17s to attack, concentrating instead on the two-seat F-105F *Wild Weasel/Iron Hand* aircraft that had quickly become an essential component in every strike formation due to the potent threat they posed to air defence SAM and AAA sites.

Phantom II CAP crews were often able to head MiG-21s off from the strike packages and pursue them, sometimes resulting in a number of successful dogfights. However, the sudden appearance of VPAF fighters behind or below an F-105 formation usually brought about the main objective of the communist pilots – to force the bombers to jettison their bomb loads and position themselves defensively. Once this had occurred a long, complex and costly USAF attack mission was negated, but F-105 pilots were still at risk of interception. Indeed, they frequently commented that the MiG combat air patrol (MiGCAP) was positioned too far away to intervene. VPAF ground controllers became adept at vectoring their fighters past the American escorts and providing them with optimum escape routes to frustrate attempts at pursuit.

The communists also learned that a single MiG could be used to attract a whole F-4 flight away from the strike force. If the MiGCAP leader chose to pursue the MiG, USAF flight integrity usually required all four Phantom IIs to go with him, allowing other VPAF aircraft access to the strike flights. These tactics contributed to the 15 Thunderchief losses to MiGs (three of them to MiG-17s) during the 18-month period of F-105 MiG kills – 12.5 less than the number of MiGs lost to Thunderchiefs. In all, F-105 pilots encountered MiGs on 151 occasions from 4 April 1965 to 1 March 1967 – more frequently than any other US aircrews. In 57 of these incidents pilots only sighted MiGs distantly and did not engage.

Some F-105 pilots completed their combat tours without seeing MiGs at all. On 17 occasions the encounters resulted in lost aircraft, and in the rest the two forces clashed without loss, although the F-105s were often forced to jettison their ordnance. Usually, this affected a few flights within the force, and by mid-1967 there were very few instances where the entire force had to jettison, sometimes because they had to fly rescue combat air patrol (RESCAP) for a downed crew.

After the dramatic events of 4 April 1965 MiGs were not seen by Takhli or Korat pilots until 24 June, when a flight of F-105Ds was pursued by two MiG-17s after bombing a bridge near Son La. Once again, fundamental problems were revealed on both sides, although on this occasion the Thunderchief pilots had the advantage of MiG warnings from an offshore *Big Eye* radar picket aircraft.

The MiGs were sighted as they closed behind the F-105s, the flight jettisoning its tanks and splitting into 'high' and 'low' elements to meet the threat. The leading MiG continued to follow the fourth F-105 (often regarded as the least experienced and most vulnerable pilot by VPAF instructors), firing at him repeatedly, but very inaccurately, in a turning fight and forcing him to escape via a Mach 1.1 dive to low altitude since the MiG was easily turning with him. The F-105 flight leader and his wingman closed on the second MiG, which was threatening the No 3 Thunderchief, but his gunsight would not acquire the target with a radar lock-on and he was able to fire very few rounds before the VPAF fighter disappeared into low cloud. He later commented on the low reliability of the radar or computer gunsights and the desirability of carrying air-to-air missiles.

There are no names attributed to the pilots involved in this particular action as USAF's records for combat engagements during the Vietnam War usually omitted crew names, using only generic colour references to identify flights and the positions of aircraft within the flights (e.g. 'Blue 02'). Where possible aircrew and actual flight names have been identified within this book. In some cases the official identity has had to be included in order to present incidents and aircrew comments that help to explain the nature of the aerial conflicts that are described. Thanks to W Howard Plunkett and Theo van Geffen for identifying some of the crew and flight names included in this volume.

Pilots frequently suggested a modification to allow a nose-wheel steering button on the control column to cancel the armament system's bombing function and instantly switch it to air-to-air mode. However, funding for F-105 updates took a low priority as the USAF was already concentrating on introducing a gun-armed F-4 Phantom II variant, and Thunderchief improvements were mainly limited to the belated provision of more survivable hydraulic systems.

The VPAF pilots attempted another interception in October 1965 when two MiG-17s chased a flight of F-105s that had completed its *Iron Hand* mission against a SAM site near Kep air base. One of the Thunderchiefs had been damaged by ground fire, but the flight could still outdistance the MiGs. Although short of fuel, it was tempting to turn and engage the enemy, but an *Iron Hand* element leader opted out of slowing down to enter a dogfight with the more manoeuvrable MiG-17 'Silver Swallows'. A similar interception occurred on 16 November when MiGs got to within three miles of a Thunderchief strike flight, which promptly accelerated to Mach 0.93 and denied the VPAF pilots a close-in fight.

The USAF's three principal Vietnam tactical fighter types are seen together at Da Nang AB in January 1967. The F-105 Thunderchief, F-100D Super Sabre and F-4C Phantom II all flew strike and MiGCAP/escort missions over North Vietnam from early in the conflict. F-105D 60-0447 previously wore the lurid sharksmouth marking of the 562nd TFS/23rd TFW in 1964, but by the time this photograph was taken the fighter had been painted in drab camouflage. On 14 April 1967 the aircraft was hit by 37 mm AAA fire during a strike on Dien Bien Phu. Its pilot, Maj Paul Craw, was rescued after being badly burned while he steered his blazing aircraft away from a village whose occupants would have certainly killed him on sight (*via Peter Schinkelshoek*)

For the rest of 1965 MiG sightings by F-105 pilots were infrequent, and there was only one attempted engagement, this time by Thunderchiefs. On 20 December a flight of F-105Ds was placed on barrier combat air patrol (BARCAP) for another flight of bomber F-105s. This was one of the occasional 'fighter' missions for Thunderchief pilots, who were normally accustomed to attack sorties. For BARCAP the aim was to set up a patrol orbit near a MiG base and prevent VPAF fighters from interfering with the strike. During that mission two MiG-17s were seen flying from Haiphong, straight, level and fast. The F-105 flight leader turned in behind the VPAF fighters and passed only 700 ft above them, but the MiG flight continued on at high speed and the BARCAP F-105s were unable to engage them.

After the unsatisfactory engagement on 4 April 1965, F-100D Super Sabres, which provided CAP during some of the early *Rolling Thunder* missions, were taken off fighter escort duties and replaced from July 1965 by F-104C Starfighters, which later specialised in escorting F-105F *Wild Weasels* on their SAM site attacks between June and August 1966. Two F-104Cs flying this close escort mission on 1 August 1966 were shot down by SAMs, probably because the aircraft had no radar warning receivers to alert them to the SA-2 missiles. The Starfighters were then replaced by F-4 Phantom IIs, but F-105s occasionally filled the CAP requirement. On some missions Thunderchief pilots bombed with the strike flights and then took up CAP positions to protect other strike flights, and on others they carried AIM-9 missiles for primary air-to-air duties.

By the end of 1965 MiG-17 pilots had taken off to intercept incoming American aircraft on 156 occasions, but they had shot down only two F-105s out of the 61 lost. VPAF pilots still had much to learn about combat tactics, effective formation flying and working within the rigid GCI framework established by their Soviet sponsors. Crucially, the successful use of GCI gave them the vital element of surprise, which was a major factor in the aerial victories claimed on both sides. Sixteen VPAF pilots had been lost since MiG-17 operations began. Although only two jets had been shot down by USAF pilots, four others had fallen to US Navy F-4 Phantom IIs, one to a pair of US Navy A-1 Skyraiders and several more had been destroyed in accidents. The USSR and China made good the losses with around 30 aircraft per year, but VPAF pilot numbers did not exceed 50 until 1966. In that year five of the casualties were caused by F-105 pilots.

President Lyndon Johnson imposed a 'bombing pause' from 24 December 1965 until the end of January 1966, but the lack of aerial opposition to F-105 activity continued until 23 April, when three MiG-17s pursued a Thunderchief that had become separated from a 388th TFW strike flight tasked with bombing the Bac Giang Bridge. The leading MiG's gunfire was scattered and missed the jet, which escaped at low altitude without afterburner. A similarly inconclusive incident occurred on 8 May, although one of the F-105 pilots was able to fire a few 20 mm rounds in response to sustained, off-target MiG cannon fire. The Thunderchief pilots concluded that the attacking VPAF flight displayed a lack of training, with the enemy pilots breaking off the fight before it could develop further. Two days later the F-105 wings lost three aircraft to AAA, and when several MiG-17s appeared the VPAF jets promptly retreated upon the arrival of an F-4 Phantom II flight.

On 29 June 1966 – the day that Maj Fred L Tracy, on his 33rd mission, made the first F-105 MiG kill – 923rd FR VPAF pilots Nguyen Van Bay (the top scoring MiG-17 ace) and Phan Van Tuc claimed F-105Ds destroyed. However, only one Thunderchief was lost in that day's massive strikes on North Vietnam's POL stores led by Maj Jim Kasler. Maj Murphy Neal Jones' 60-0460 was reportedly hit by 85 mm AAA, but Phan Van Tuc's gun camera film was the VPAF's evidence that he was shot down by a MiG-17. This frame shows an F-105D, allegedly Jones', with its air-brakes extended and afterburner lit up. Three other F-105Ds were damaged during the mission (*via Dr István Toperczer*)

FIRST KILL

Although it could not appear in official records, the first MiG kill by an F-105D happened at the end of a 25-mile chase into Chinese airspace on 10 May 1966. It was one of several similar incidents involving US fighters and fleeing VPAF, or Chinese communist MiGs, and it caused increased policing of US air activity in the northern border areas of North Vietnam by EC-121D airborne radar surveillance aircraft.

The year was half gone before F-105 crews finally had an official chance to avenge their losses to MiG-17s 14 months previously. On 29 June Maj James Kasler, operations officer of the 354th TFS, led 46 F-105s from both wings in a new campaign to hit petrol, oil and lubricant (POL) storage sites, bombing unprecedentedly close to Hanoi. 'Crab' flight from the 421st TFS/388th TFW provided *Iron Hand* SAM suppression for the attack, and it had just destroyed a SAM site with AGM-45 Shrike missiles and Mk 4 Folding-Fin Aerial Rockets fired from LAU-3A launchers when four MiG-17s began to close in behind at around 5000 ft as the flight rejoined the strike force at 480 knots. 'Crab 4' belatedly saw them heading in and broadcast a warning that the lead 'Crab' element one mile ahead apparently did not hear. 'Crab 3' (Maj Kenneth D Frank) and '4' made a diving turn, with gunfire from the leading MiG following them but missing 'Crab 3'.

The MiGs pressed on, lining up on the lead 'Crab' element just as 'Crab 1' (an F-105F flown by Maj Richard D Westcott and Capt Herbert L Friesen) saw them. He called for afterburner and the jettisoning of ordnance, after which his element broke sharply to the left. Nine 23 mm and 37 mm cannon shells hit Maj Fred Tracy's 'Crab 2' (F-105D 58-1156). One of the 23 mm projectiles forced the pilot's hand away from the throttle, abruptly cancelling his afterburner. It also knocked out most of Tracy's cockpit instruments, large areas of the left cockpit interior, the oxygen equipment and gunsight. The projectile then lodged in his AC power pack, fortunately without exploding.

As the F-105 slowed without afterburner the MiG overshot and Tracy fired 200 rounds of 20 mm ammunition without the aid of a gunsight. 'I manoeuvred to superimpose my pitot boom over the MiG, squeezed the trigger and saw the 20 mm rounds sparkling along the left fuselage and wing root of the MiG. His left wing folded over the tail and in an abrupt left turn he went into a cloud at about 2500 ft'. Maj Tracy saw about ten definite hits. Intelligence sources later discovered MiG-17 wreckage and confirmed that the fighter had crashed. Tracy, who was on the mission to check out a new *Wild Weasel* pilot, became the first F-105 MiG killer.

All four 'Crab' flight pilots were involved in the dogfight. The lead F-105 was hit in its tail surfaces by the second MiG, and would have been further damaged had Maj Frank not fired at it, forcing the VPAF pilot to abandon his firing pass. All pilots then fired at the enemy aircraft, including a 200-round burst from 'Crab 4', but only Tracy's bullets are known to have struck home. His skill (and luck) enabled him to shoot the MiG down without a gunsight, but the pilots involved in the next dogfight were less fortunate.

A 388th TFW flight bombed a target near Hanoi and had split into two elements when a SAM almost hit one of them. Sighting two MiG-17s a short while later, the second element leader used afterburner to pursue the communist fighters until he opened fire from 1000 ft above them. Both Thunderchief pilots expended more than 200 rounds each, but the MiGs saw their approach and made hard turns to avoid the gunfire. The F-105s were also unable to make their radar gunsights lock onto the targets (one was apparently locking onto ground returns). They were

Maj Fred Tracy and 1Lt Karl Richter hold the '100 F-105 Missions over North Vietnam' flag. Richter's name was painted on the canopy of Tracy's MiG killer F-105D (58-1156) for publicity photos, although Richter's 100th mission was actually flown in his own MiG-killing F-105D, 59-1766. The initial deployment of F-105 pilots included many with backgrounds in fighters and F-105 experience from McConnell AFB. By mid-1966 the majority had completed their tours and been replaced by instructor pilots from Nellis AFB and the two USAFE Thunderchief wings. Among them was Maj Tracy, who took over the 421st TFS at Korat from Lt Col Barnett and soon became a well-liked leader. He revived the tradition of giving each pilot his 'own' aircraft with his name on the canopy (*USAF*)

eventually forced to make a 5g turn away from the MiGs and disengage while they still had a speed advantage, rather than entering a turning fight.

As the year progressed VPAF pilots' tactics developed. They realised that F-105s were particularly vulnerable as they climbed away from their targets after bombing because pilots had left their usual defensive formations in order to perform their individual attacks. Pilots were also concentrating fully on getting bombs on target during their dive attacks, with little time to make the switch changes to engage their air-to-air weapons as they pulled out, while also trying to rejoin their flights and exit the target area. MiG pilots would therefore try to 'jump' the F-105s at that moment, as they did on 7 July. Four MiG-17s went for the second element in a strike flight, but the F-105 pilots reacted by turning back into the enemy fighters, which promptly vanished into smoky haze.

Thunderchief pilots found that they were at their most vulnerable during the last three minutes before their ordnance delivery and the first minute or two afterwards. The communist defenders were able to coordinate their MiGs, SAMs and AAA most effectively at those times, avoiding the risk of shooting down their own fighters. Conventional Soviet doctrine put the MiG screen out ahead of the SAM belts, but over North Vietnam the two generally worked well together.

Another favourite tactic was to concentrate attacks by MiG-21s on the high-value *Iron Hand* and *Wild Weasel* flights that softened up enemy defences ahead of the strike force. A two-ship *Iron Hand* flight preceded the 7 July strike package and a pair of MiG-21s intercepted it. The lead 388th TFW F-105F attempted to engage one of them, but the MiG was faster and easily turned inside the F-105F, firing two 'Atoll' air-to-air missiles at it, which missed. The F-105D wingman also tried to engage the VPAF jets but he was unable to manage the complex switching sequence to jettison his ordnance and activate his cannon in time. He had to escape in afterburner 'on the deck'. By that time the F-105F crew had reached 650 knots at low altitude, and after losing sight of the MiG they chose to expend their last Shrike missile on another SAM site, instead of continuing the engagement with the enemy jet.

The M118 3049-lb bomb, 18 ft in length, was the main choice for hard targets like bridges. Within TAC only the A-1 Skyraider and F-105 were capable of employing the bomb, with the Thunderchief being restricted to carrying it on its inboard 'special weapons' pylons. Upon detonation, the M118 created a huge shockwave, and pilots had to be sure to avoid its effects. MiG killer Karl Richter had a stabilator blown off by an M118 blast, while other pilots experienced severe asymmetric control problems when one of the bombs failed to release. Mk 82 'Lady Fingers' 500-lb bombs were often used on *Iron Hand* missions. Two M117 or Mk 82 bombs could also be loaded on the outboard pylons for missions over Laos, where ECM pods were not required (*USAF*)

Their ability to fight the MiG-21 on this occasion was impeded by another unforeseen difficulty in operating the F-105 at high speeds in such humid climatic conditions. At one point the wingman's visibility was so limited by thick condensation on the aircraft's canopy that he had to slow down and let it clear. The condensation started at the rear of the canopy and worked its way forward with increasing airspeed until only vision through the windscreen panels was possible.

Lack of visibility of a different kind could work to the F-105 pilots' advantage, however. Camouflage paint was applied to the aircraft during 1966, and on one 11 July mission a flight of Thunderchiefs armed with massive 3000-lb M118 'bridge-busting' bombs blended in so well with the landscape at an altitude of just 50 ft near the VPAF air base at Kep that they were not noticed by a passing MiG-17 patrol. On this occasion the USAF pilots were under orders to keep their M118s aboard unless they were directly attacked by the VPAF fighters. Fuel tanks were normally jettisoned if MiGs engaged the F-105 formation, and if one of them failed to drop the asymmetric configuration made the aircraft difficult to control at speeds above 500 knots.

Many MiG-17s were also painted in various camouflage schemes during 1966 in an attempt to improve the chances of their 'hi-lo' interception tactic resulting in the destruction of American aircraft. Maj 'Ted' Tolman (355th TFW weapons officer in July 1967) spotted a camouflaged MiG-17 shortly after he and his wingman had completed their bombing run. They closed in behind the VPAF jet just as it in turn started threatening his flight lead element. However, the enemy pilot turned sharply away when he saw the two F-105s behind him;

'I called flight lead and said the MiG had turned away from his tail and he could slow down. At that moment a MiG dropped in behind me. They like to keep one or two aircraft at a medium altitude and another element at an extremely low altitude, but within sight of the high element. I'm sure that many of the MiGs were camouflaged this day. They put two or three right down on the deck, which effectively hid them from view from an attacking pilot who would see the high element and go after them, allowing the low element to jump up behind the attacking aircraft.'

NEAR MISSES

The elusive second MiG kill was not achieved until 18 August, but it was preceded by some more near misses and continuing, frustrating technical problems. Several were highlighted during another *Iron Hand* fracas with MiG-21s on 21 July, when four Takhli-based aircraft were returning individually from a successful SAM suppression mission and egressing along the low Tam Dao mountain range known as 'Thud Ridge'. As they attempted to rejoin the flight the No 2 F-105 pilot, Maj W L McClelland, saw two aircraft about four miles ahead of him and accelerated to join up with them, assuming that they were his flight members. A radio check with his flight leader confirmed the *Iron Hand* aircrafts' general heading.

At a distance of 2000 ft McClelland realised that the fighters did not look much like F-105s, and he also noticed that his gunsight was not set up. Suddenly, one of the aircraft pulled up sharply to the right, revealing red VPAF markings on its MiG-21 wings. McClelland executed a quick 180-degree turn, jettisoned his stores and headed north. Shortly afterwards, as he rolled out of the turn, he noticed a MiG-21 canopy-to-canopy but just ahead of him. McClelland turned towards it, running at supersonic speed with most of his instruments inoperative. Condensation fogged his canopy so he could not determine whether or not he had lost the MiG-21.

McClelland continued 'on the deck' and found a valley leading out of 'Thud Ridge' that took him west across the Red River. Only then did he come out of afterburner and zoom climb to find a tanker, as he was down to 2000 lbs of fuel. Sadly, the airwaves were jammed with other aircraft seeking tankers and his IFF (Identification, Friend or Foe) was not working. Just as he saw a tanker ahead of him his engine flamed out and he had to eject, leaving F-105D 61-0121 to crash into the Laotian jungle. Three MiG-21 pilots claimed this as a kill.

In the same flight the fourth *Iron Hand* pilot also had an interesting fight. With an inoperative radio and low fuel indications that meant he had to keep re-setting a circuit breaker to make the aircraft's bomb-bay fuel tank feed the fuel system, he saw two MiG-21s turning towards his 'four o'clock' position to intercept. He cleaned off his external stores and dived in afterburner, before turning to meet one of the MiGs head-on. The VPAF jet made a steep climbing turn, which he followed and eventually barrel-rolled into a position behind it, but broke off because of his uncertain fuel situation.

The tables were turned seconds later when he banked to check behind him and saw the second MiG-21 in a perfect firing position on his tail. He engaged the 'burner again and made a hard descending turn just as the MiG pilot fired two 'Atolls', which passed him without detonating. Undeterred, he completed the manoeuvre and placed his aircraft on the MiG's tail. Awareness of his parlous fuel situation prevailed, and he chose to break off and head for Udorn RTAFB, constantly re-setting the fuel circuit breaker and finally landing with only 200 lbs of fuel remaining.

A bigger dogfight developed on 19 July involving eight F-105s and four MiG-17s, three of which were damaged. The MiG-17 pilots' confidence was clearly increasing, judging by their greater willingness to engage with the strike forces. Newly trained MiG-21 pilots also arrived in greater numbers during June and July, and they too became more formidable opponents. Revised tactics were used in which MiG-21s awaited the US aircraft at high altitude, ready to make supersonic dive attacks, while the MiG-17s patrolled below 5000 ft.

A 19 July *Rolling Thunder* mission by 16 F-105s took them to a fuel storage target north of Hanoi across intense SAM and AAA fire, bearing heavy loads of Mk 84 and M118 bombs, CBU-24 canisters (the so-called 'chopper' load-out) and, in one case, a bulky combat camera pod. Three MiG-17s approached the first F-105 flight (led by Maj Jim Kasler) from behind, just short of the target, forcing them to jettison their loads as the enemy fighters opened fire. They turned to face the MiGs, and the second element leader fired a burst at 90 degrees deflection that caused the VPAF jet to trail smoke and debris from its wing. As the only pilot in the flight with air-to-air missiles aboard, he then selected an AIM-9B and fired at the departing aircraft, but the weapon failed to guide. A second missile also missed, having possibly been fired outside of its g-limits. He then reverted to the gun once again, but the MiG dived sharply and the Thunderchief pilots lost sight of it.

With their ordnance still aboard the second F-105 flight continued on to their target. Meanwhile, the first two 355th TFW pilots, Jim Kasler and 1Lt Steve Diamond, were involved in a dogfight with two 923rd FR MiG-17s flown by Nguyen Bien and Vo Van Man that lasted for almost 20 minutes. This engagement explored many of the tactics in the fighter pilot's air combat manoeuvring manual, including the Lufbery circle, scissors, yo-yo and maximum power turns. Kasler used all of his fighter experience from World War 2 and Korea to avoid the MiGs' cannon shells in at least seven firing passes, engaging and disengaging afterburner and turning more tightly by using his leading-edge flaps. Their altitude dropped from 7000 ft to well below 500 ft and their speed was falling steadily during the high-energy manoeuvres, with MiG-17s glued to their 'six o'clock' positions.

Crowded UHF communications (the entire strike force, together with US Navy and ECM aircraft in the area, were using the same radio frequency) meant that the MiGCAP fighters never heard Kasler's calls for help. None of the F-105 flights had heard MiG warnings for the same reason. Assistance finally came from the four F-105s of the second attack flight, which intervened as they returned from the target. Two of its aircraft made a diving gun attack on the MiGs without scoring hits, and then as they climbed and turned for a second attack they lost sight of the VPAF fighters.

The two beleaguered F-105 pilots then called for help from their own second element as it too returned from the target, but before they could intervene gunfire from Vo Van Man's MiG-17 mortally hit Diamond's Thunderchief (59-1755). As he closed for a second attack Vo Van Man was in turn hit by Maj Kasler, who had closed in behind the MiG, damaging its tail. Kasler then saw the VPAF pilot turn away and head for

F-105s usually carried only a solitary AIM-9B Sidewinder, as the remaining four pylons were required for fuel tanks, bomb racks or an ECM pod (*Don Larsen*)

AIM-9Bs ready for uploading to an F-105D. A successful launch of a Sidewinder inside very tight launch parameters against a manoeuvring target was difficult to achieve, and the F-105's single air-to-air missile compared with eight carried by the F-4 Phantom II dictated the use of the M61A1 cannon on most occasions when MiGs had to be tackled (*USAF*)

Phuc Yen airfield, and he pursued the MiG in afterburner, hoping to finish it off. Heavy AAA from the base and the knowledge that MiGs could not be attacked at their airfields at that time forced him to turn for home. Moments later Kasler's F-105 was damaged by fire from Nguyen Bien's MiG, which had appeared behind him.

Meanwhile, the leader of the second F-105 flight and his wingman (who had sustained AAA damage over the target) arrived over Phuc Yen, determined to shoot Bien's MiG-17 off Kasler's tail. The element leader closed in for a gun attack, although his wingman was configured for air-to-air with two AIM-9Bs (he later stated that he 'did what was natural', i.e. choosing a gunnery pass over missiles). He opened fire at 3000 ft and kept firing until he was within 50 ft, almost ramming the MiG. Hit in its right wing, the MiG made a 6g left turn that the F-105 was unable to follow. As Kasler broke free of the fight, his Nos 3 and 4 flight-members also appeared over the airfield and engaged a fourth MiG-17 in Nguyen Bien's flight, firing at it as they thundered across the airfield at 500 ft. At that point the storm of 37 mm AAA rising from the airfield obliged them to leave the area, but not before one of the F-105s had been damaged by flak.

During this, the longest aerial engagement in the war up to that time, Steven Diamond was shot down by Vo Van Man and ejected, but his subsequent fate was never established. The experience reinforced awareness of the ongoing communications problems for the strike forces, the superior manoeuvrability of the MiG-17 and the difficulty in using AIM-9Bs successfully in a turning fight. Pilots still regarded the M61A1 as their first-call weapon for MiG engagements. Above all, this fight showed that F-105 pilots could exploit their fighter's air-to-air capability to the full when given the opportunity.

They were given another chance on 20 July when five separate sightings and engagements occurred during strike missions in Route Pack VIA, although in each case the VPAF pilots made single passes at F-105 flights near their targets and then dived away. In one encounter that day a MiG-21 approached a strike flight from the left and the Thunderchief pilots jettisoned their drop tanks and split into high and low elements, hoping to 'box' the fighter in. The MiG pilot, seeing the tanks falling away, probably assumed that he had achieved his objective of making the F-105s jettison their ordnance and he broke off his attack. The 'Thud' pilots flew on and bombed their target.

GUNS AND GUNSIGHTS

22 July marked one of the F-105's earliest encounters with the VPAF's MiG-17PF (ten of which were delivered at the end of 1965) and its missiles. The fighter's 37 mm gun had been replaced by a third 23 mm weapon and an RP-5 Izumrud-2 'Scan Rod' gun-aiming radar that had a detection range of up to five miles and auto-tracking for the guns at one mile, useable below 2.5gs. Two of the attacking MiG-17PFs fired unguided air-to-air rockets at the strike flight, but these were easily evaded via a rapid left break into clouds. Emerging from the cloud-base, the second F-105 element leader, a Korean War veteran, saw one of the MiGs approaching head-on and fired more than 100 rounds of 20 mm ammunition at it without result before losing sight of the fighter.

The aerial campaign against North Vietnam's POL reserves intensified in August 1966, and F-105 losses mounted accordingly. Two 333rd TFS 'Lancers' aircraft were shot down by AAA on 12 August, one over the massive Thai Nguyen industrial complex and a second, flown by Capt David Allinson, while strafing trucks on the way back. Pilots from both the F-105 flights involved set up a RESCAP for Capt Allinson – an event that often attracted MiGs to disturb the recovery effort.

Two MiG-17s soon appeared, the F-105s responded and an extended 'furball' ensued. Four pilots fired more than 2000 rounds at the MiGs and probably damaged two, although the gun cameras that could have confirmed this were inoperable. One of the Thunderchiefs took a hit in the top of its left wing, but it fought on. Time and again, the MiG pilots avoided F-105 gunfire by using their superior turning ability just as the American pilots achieved a favourable firing solution. AIM-9Bs were carried but not used, and the pilots reported that the missiles were in poor condition, with scratched, pitted seeker heads. The RESCAP was abandoned when it was clear that Allinson was unable to make radio contact with the rescuers and was presumed dead.

A 333rd TFS F-105D, with a flak suppression ordnance load-out, takes on fuel. Refuelling orbits were colour-coded – e.g. 'Blue Anchor', with the 'anchor' part indicating the two fixed 'anchor' points, one at each end of the 40-mile long track offshore or over Laos. Fully loaded F-105Ds were limited to around 18,000 ft for in-flight refuelling at around 315 knots from the 'high' tanker of the five usually allocated to each strike formation. The other tankers were staggered at lower altitudes. Cruising at around 95 per cent power, a loaded F-105 burned 600 gallons per hour, which increased to 150 gallons per minute on takeoff (*via Peter Schinkelshoek*)

The VPAF employed its established tactic of attacking F-105s coming off target once again on 17 August. A Korat-based flight, reduced to two aircraft by unserviceable radios, made its bomb run on a target near Hanoi and the lead aircraft collected a MiG-17 on his tail as he pulled up. His wingman, close behind, was accelerating to catch up with the MiG when he saw flames flashing from its guns. He in turn hastily fired a brief burst, using the centre of his windscreen as a gunsight as he had not had time to switch on the real thing. This 'World War 1' approach served several F-105 pilots well, but on this occasion there were no hits. The flight leader, meanwhile, descended to an estimated altitude of just five feet, pulling up to avoid the low dikes around rice fields, and accelerated to Mach 1.2 to escape the lone MiG's persistent gun fire.

The following day brought better fortune. Sixteen Korat aircraft, including an *Iron Hand* flight, hit a POL installation north of Hanoi. The *Iron Hand* flight ('Honda') became separated into elements when it had to avoid a heavy thunderstorm, but the leading pair found their SAM site target. Two SA-2 missiles were launched at them and one exploded between the two Thunderchiefs, 'blowing out' the afterburner of 'Honda 2'. Majs 'Robbie' Robinson and Pete Tsouprake, in F-105F 'Honda 1', fired two AGM-45 Shrike missiles at a SAM site and then had to jettison their rocket pods and centreline fuel tank when, without warning, two MiG-17s were seen by the following 'Schlitz' F-105 flight to be closing on their tail.

Encountering MiGs in an environment where SAMs were the principal defence was unusual at the time. Indeed, it was Robinson's 50th *Wild Weasel* mission, but the first during which he had met MiGs. His F-105F sustained only one hit on the vertical stabiliser and another that grazed the wing. Maj Kenneth T Blank from the 34th TFS was his wingman in F-105D 60-0458 'Honda 2', and he heard Robinson call, 'Get him off my ass!' His wingman instructed Robinson to break left, and he passed beneath Blank's F-105 with the MiG still shooting at him. 'Honda 2' quickly got rid of his two drop tanks and rocket pods and moved into the MiG's 'six o'clock' position.

In the heat of the moment, even with 153 missions in Korea and Vietnam and 600 hrs on the F-105 under his belt, Blank found the jet's daunting armament switching sequence impossible to manage in time. Closing to within 500 ft of the VPAF fighter

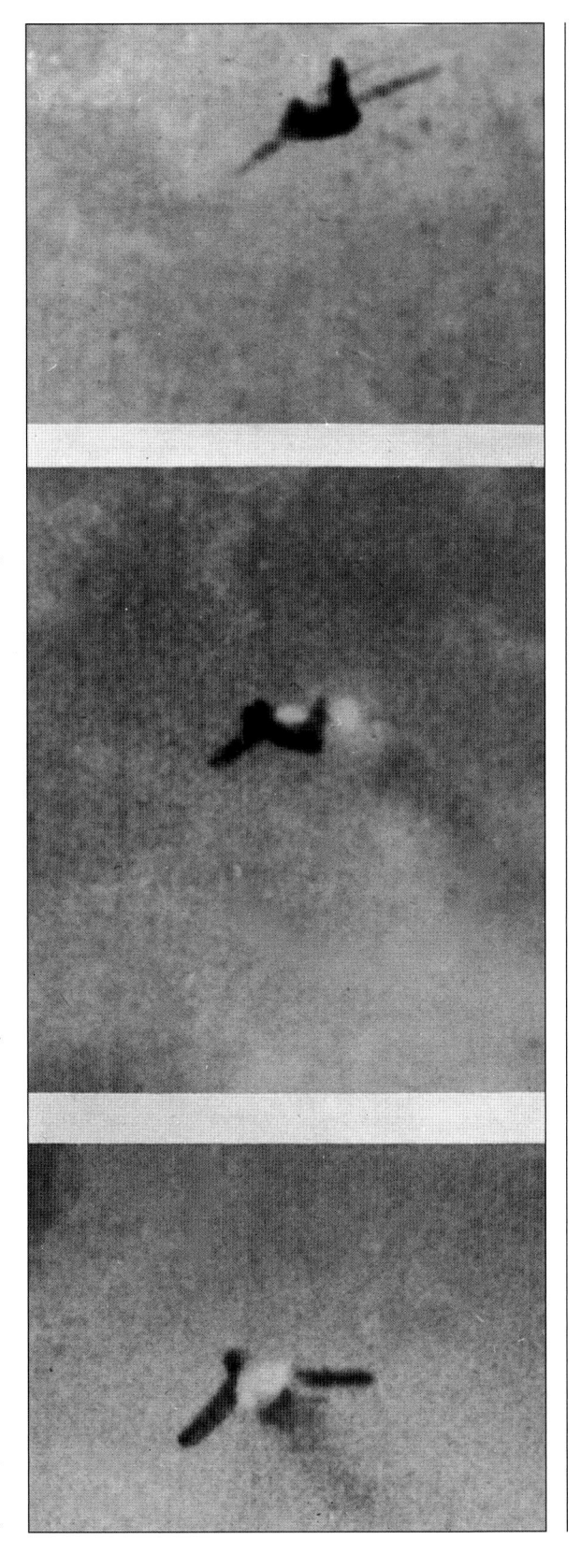

Opposite:
The second F-105 pilot to shoot down a MiG-17 was Maj Kenneth T Blank. On 18 August 1966, as 'Honda 2', he closed to within 500 ft of a VPAF fighter that was shooting at 'Honda' flight leader, Maj Robbie Robinson, and fired without the use of a gunsight. Assigned to the 34th TFS as a replacement pilot on 2 June 1966, Maj Blank completed 100 missions and went on to command the 55th TFS/20th TFW in England. He was killed in the crash of one of its F-111Es in January 1972 (*DoD*)

so that it filled his windscreen, he fired 216 rounds without the aid of a gunsight. The MiG burst into flames, flipped over and dived into the ground in a fireball that was seen by the following 'Manila' F-105 flight.

'Manila 2' also fired at a MiG-17, using the pitot boom 'gunsight', but no hits were seen and the flight exited down 'Thud Ridge' with three VPAF jets in hot pursuit.

Vietnamese records show that Capt Pham Thanh Chung was the only MiG pilot lost that day. Blank reported his regret at the F-105 weapons system's lack of ranging information and his wish for better early warning of MiG activity. He also repeated the increasingly familiar complaints about the F-105's armament 'switchology' and restricted turning capability. Placing the MiG in the centre of the F-105's windscreen was an idea that Blank had picked up from Capt Doug Lauck, who had chased a MiG-17 that was pursuing his 'Anvil' flight leader the previous day (17 August). Without time to re-set his armament switches for air-to-air, Lauck centred the MiG in his windshield and fired 75 rounds at it, but he had had to break off his pursuit when the VPAF pilot crossed the Chinese border.

Maj Blank was not alone in his frustration with the gunsight problem that day. A wingman in the last two-aircraft flight to hit the Hanoi area targets watched Blank's victim falling in a fiery trail, but he then noticed, without warning, more MiGs threatening his own flight. One of them came out of low cloud about 1000 ft ahead of his aircraft, clearly going for the lead F-105D. Lacking a functioning gunsight, the Thunderchief pilot used his pitot boom 'gunsight' and fired 184 rounds at the MiG without seeing hits. As pulled up to get a better angle on the jet, three more MiGs latched onto the tail of his flight leader, who became aware of their presence when numerous tracer bullets passed by his canopy. The only solution to this problem was to rely on the J75's afterburner once again, the F-105 diving away and disengaging from the VPAF fighters.

Another common source of missed MiG kill opportunities was experienced by a 388th TFW flight on 22 August. The pilots had just bombed a secondary target and were rejoining formation when they were bounced by four MiG-17s, again without warning from the *Big Eye* radar picket. Luckily, the No 3 pilot noticed MiGs closing fast from behind, firing at them. One F-105 had the top six inches of its tailfin blasted off and another took hits in its right wing flap. Two pilots were able to turn and fire at the pursuers, which caused two MiG-17s to disengage. The F-105 flight leader had the best chance of a hit on a MiG that was chasing the fourth man in the flight. He fired 150 rounds but then his gun jammed. He called in the F-104C MiGCAP, orbiting to the north, but the message was not received.

Jammed guns were a fairly common occurrence in most contemporary fighters. Excessive g-forces, loading errors or rushed maintenance could all be causes, but all too often problems seemed to occur just as a pilot had a real chance of a kill. Many also bemoaned the lack of F-105 air combat training. The second pilot in the 22 August flight, who had almost 2000 hrs on fighters extending back to the F-86 Sabre and 80 combat missions to his credit, reported that his only air combat manoeuvring (ACM) training on the F-105 had been through unofficial practice within the squadron and reading the MiG-17 flight manual. The Thunderchief's nuclear strike training legacy lived on.

CHAPTER THREE

FRANTIC FIGHTS

From 4 September 1966 to early January 1967 MiGs were sighted virtually every day, and there was a marked increase in their aggression and improved coordination of their GCI network. September 1966 saw numerous heated engagements between the two F-105 wings and the VPAF, leading to the third MiG kill on the 21st. In the first fight, on 9 September, MiG-21s appeared behind an *Iron Hand* flight without warning, again because all the aircraft concerned were flying below the radar coverage of the EC-121 *Big Eye/Ethan Alpha* radar aircraft. The lead F-105 pilot was able to position himself behind one of the MiGs and fire 600 rounds in two bursts without result, before leaving the scene at 650 knots just 100 ft above a valley floor. The MiGs followed, but soon turned back.

Two MiG-17s sought to disrupt another 388th TFW *Iron Hand* flight on 14 September over the Dap Cau railway bridge. They latched onto the F-105 flight leader as he left the target, but the Thunderchief pilot accelerated away from them. His wingman closed in behind the MiGs, flying through barrage 85 mm AAA to reach them. He opened fire, but after only six rounds a shear pin failed and the gun stopped working. Again, no MiG warning was received, but the F-105s used their speed to escape.

Members of a 388th TFW strike flight attacking the same target were also intercepted by MiG-17s after they had dropped 3000-lb bombs and CBU-24s on the bridge. One of the F-105 pilots, on his first combat tour, jettisoned his wing pylons and managed to close to within a mile of a MiG-17. He had almost attained a good firing position when the VPAF pilot made a sudden, sharp turn and was very soon in a position to make a head-on pass at the F-105, but he elected to break off and head for Kep air base instead. Just as the F-105 flight was about to complete a join-up over the coast 1Lt R J Casper's F-105D (62-4306) was hit by 57 mm AAA, which removed half of the jet's right wing. Casper ejected and was recovered for the second time in six weeks. His colleagues noted that he had shaved off his 'bullet-proof' moustache the previous night, confirming their deeply held superstitions on that subject.

MiGs were encountered again on 15 and 16 September, and on the second occasion the F-105 flights jettisoned ordnance and briefly engaged them, firing one snapshot burst before the VPAF fighters departed with their work done. Another Korat F-105 flight on the same mission saw three MiGs at very low altitude waiting to climb and attack them from the rear. The flight leader decided to try and turn in behind the MiGs to execute a tactic whereby he would pursue the third enemy jet while his own second element trapped another one between them. Sadly, his message to engage the MiGs was blocked by radio interference, and just as he accelerated to within gun range of 'his' quarry it made a sudden left turn. The MiGs then had the advantage, and the F-105 leader called in the MiGCAP F-4s, which announced that they had to leave the area due to fuel shortage. The F-105 flight therefore had to depart as fast as possible too.

Phantom IIs had only recently started to escort the strike force directly, rather than flying patrol orbits, and the speed differences between the faster F-105s and themselves gave F-4 crews unexpected fuel management problems.

A similarly rapid exit was required on 17 September in a raid on bridges northeast of Kep by 388th TFW aircraft. The flight leader, Capt Darel Leetun, was hit by AAA as he left the target and he was lost in the subsequent crash of his F-105D (62-4280). The second element in the flight headed for the coast, but Leetun's wingman, Capt Mike Lanning, became separated and strayed into Chinese airspace, partly because his aircraft had an inoperative horizontal situation indicator. Chinese People's Liberation Army Air Force J-6s (locally-built MiG-19s) immediately attacked him, Lanning spotting cannon fire blazing past both wings. He hastily entered a split-S manoeuvre and managed to escape at low altitude by using his afterburner just as the J-6s made a second gun-firing pass at him.

Aggressive approaches by VPAF MiG-17s the following day caused two flights of Korat F-105s to jettison their ordnance and another to abandon its attack and drop short of the target. A fourth flight, with M118s, was able to continue to its Dap Cau railway bridge target only by descending to 50 ft in afterburner. The MiGs turned back when this strike element entered an area of heavy 85 mm AAA fire. Only one of the flights was fired at, and all the MiGs left as soon as their pilots saw the American ordnance fall away harmlessly.

More intense fights took place on 20 September as the F-105s continued with the bridge and highway attack stage of *Rolling Thunder*. Three flights were targeted by four MiG-17s, and one of the F-105s had to leave 'on the deck' as a hung 1000-lb bomb prevented the pilot from manoeuvring with the enemy fighters. The three F-4C Phantom II MiGCAP aircraft cleaned off their drop tanks, ready to fight, but were unable to locate the

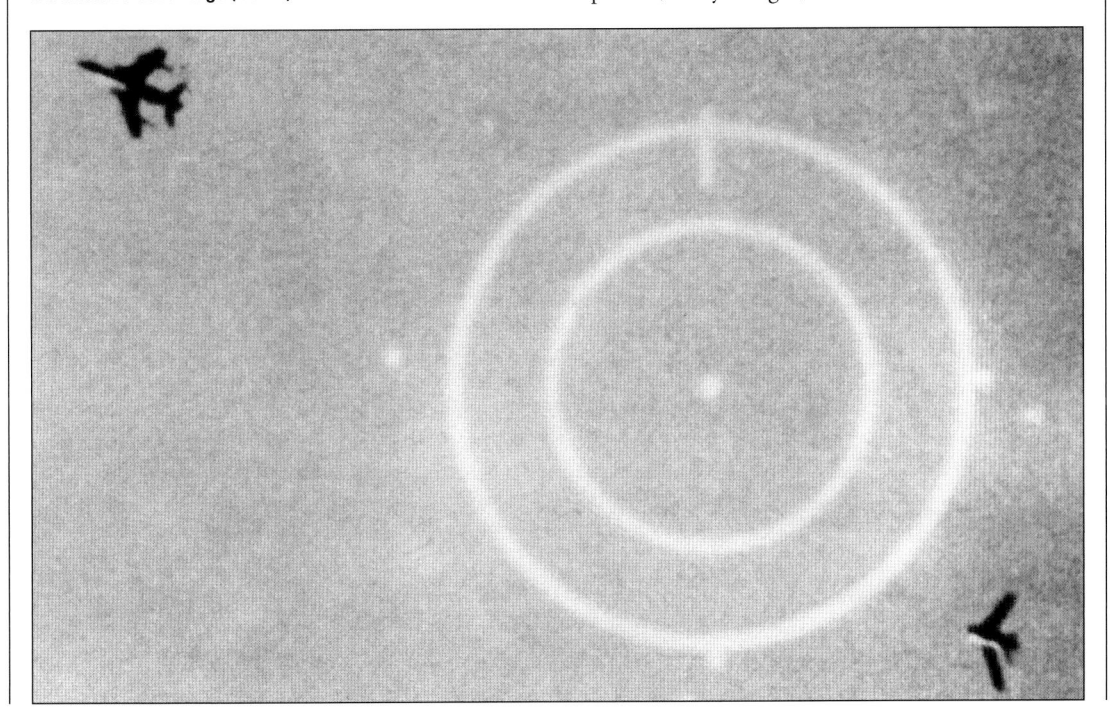

A Thunderchief's gun camera frame that only hints at the gut-wrenching life and death duel taking place between a MiG-17 and another F-105D. Turning with MiG-17s in an aircraft that was as long as a B-24 Liberator (but with more bombs and ten fewer crew members) required precise judgement to know when to disengage and accelerate away before the adversary could get on the Thunderchief's tail. F-105 pilots could not easily employ the tactic used by F-4 crews, which sought to draw MiG-17s into a vertical fight where the Phantom II's superior thrust gave it a decisive advantage (*USAF*)

VPAF jets. Three MiG-17s fired at the US aircraft and three members of the 'Whisper' *Iron Hand* flight (led by Maj William P Robinson, with EWO Capt Peter Tsouprake, 1Lt Maxie A Hatcher Jr (No 2), Maj James W O'Neil with EWO Capt George E Kennedy (No 3) and Capt Michael D Thomas in the No 4 slot) fired back at them, but no hits were registered by either side. The lead crew leader had the best chance, but Maj Robinson inadvertently re-set his armament system from 'bombs' to 'rockets'. With the wrong sight depression setting dialled in, his subsequent bursts of 460 rounds all missed. Another 'Whisper' pilot fired more than 200 rounds, 'stirring' the control column to spread the bullets as his gunsight reticle was not working, but he also missed.

As the *Iron Hand* leader later stated on record after this clash;

'The F-105 needs a quick, sure method to select guns-air. It is a good aircraft for this type of war, but any new aircraft should be able to manoeuvre in high-g conditions. The F-105 can fight with the MiG-21 at low altitudes according to Maj John Boyd's Energy Manoeuvrability Charts [Boyd's study revolutionised USAF views on air combat tactics]. It can hassle with MiGs in clean configuration with less than 5000 lb of fuel. It needs tracer ammunition in the guns. The gunsight camera also needs to be improved as it currently produces hazy images.'

With more than two years on Air Defence Command F-101 and F-102 fighters, Robinson had plenty of relevant experience, but for those who lacked this background he also commented, 'Combat is a tough place to learn what a pilot must know to survive in engagements with enemy fighters'.

The dogfights of 20-21 September comprised the first large-scale aerial battle of the war, with substantial numbers of MiGs involved. On 20 September a Korat-based *Iron Hand* flight was once again at the centre of the first scrap of the day. Warned of MiGs as they headed for their target, they saw two other Thunderchiefs with a MiG-21 2000 ft behind them. The *Iron Hand* F-105F crew dumped their ordnance (including some AGM-45 Shrike missiles) and moved in behind the MiG-21, whose controller ordered him to make a 'turn on a dime' 180-degree reversal that placed him virtually head-on to the USAF jets. The F-105F pilot fired 120 rounds at it but his gun then jammed. Two of the other F-105Ds in the flight, their canopies partly obscured by condensation, engaged a second MiG-21, entering a series of semi-scissors manoeuvres with it without either side gaining the advantage. The MiGs then broke away and the *Iron Hand* pilots pursued them for several minutes before having to turn back and find a tanker.

At the time of his MiG-17 shoot down on 21 September 1966, 23-year-old 1Lt Karl Richter from Holly, Michigan, was the youngest pilot to have destroyed a MiG in Vietnam. He was killed in action on 28 July 1967 when shot down by AAA while attacking a bridge in the mountains west of Dong Hoi on his 198th mission (the high time record for the F-105). Richter's bond with the Thunderchief was strong, stating 'It even gives me a thrill to taxi that F-105'. He had planned to complete 200 Thunderchief missions and then do a tour as an F-100F Super Sabre forward air control pilot. The voluble, good-humoured Richter was acknowledged as a natural fighter pilot who always enjoyed 'working at 100 per cent capacity'. Prior to his death Richter had stated that he wanted to apply his combat experience ('a sort of PhD in professional weapons') to a career as an instructor (*USAF*)

1Lt Karl Richter with Capt Ralph Beardsley, his wingman ('Ford 4') for his MiG kill on 21 September 1966. Thailand's heat and humidity necessitated a daily change of flight suit, and 'suiting up' could take 15 minutes to complete. An under-arm holster held a Smith & Wesson .38 Combat Masterpiece firearm. For overwater flight an inflatable life preserver was also housed in under-arm pouches (*USAF*)

On the same day a Takhli flight, returning from yet another Dap Cau mission, rescued an F-4C Phantom II crew with a black, green and red painted MiG-17 on their tail that was closing fast for a good firing opportunity. The F-105 flight leader manoeuvred behind the MiG and followed it down to an altitude of 300 ft, firing 568 rounds of 20 mm ammunition in several long bursts while the F-4 crew remained apparently unaware of their pursuer! The MiG disappeared into the 'Hanoi haze', but two of the F-105 pilots saw the flashes of bullets exploding on its right wing. An incorrect gunsight setting was again responsible for the lack of decisive damage to the enemy fighter.

However, the Dap Cau battle was far from over, and two MiGs fell to F-105 pilots before it had ended. Another Korat *Iron Hand* flight, 'Ford', achieved the first victory during the 21 September attacks. The leader, in an F-105F, had just fired a Shrike at a SAM site and was turning back for another shot, while the second 'Ford' element was following the first missile to see if it hit, when Capt Ralph Beardsley ('Ford 4') detected a pair of MiG-17s closing in behind the lead Thunderchief.

As 1Lt Karl Richter ('Ford 3') set up his switches for 'guns-air', the F-105F crew and their wingman F-105D shed their drop tanks but retained their ordnance and kept the MiGs 4000 ft behind them for Richter's element to attack. 'Ford' leader called to Richter, 'I'll hold him here if you can get on him'. Richter's F-105D element jettisoned their 650-gallon tanks and LAU-3 rocket pods, but Richter's tank would not let go. Both pilots went to afterburner and cut off the MiGs as they turned away from the lead F-105F. Karl Richter fired two bursts from a range of 2000 ft and saw pieces of the MiG's right wing fly off. The pilot, Do Huy Hoang, rolled level and lit his afterburner as his MiG began to roll uncontrollably to the right. His wingman turned away sharply and Capt Beardsley had a quick shot at it without seeing hits.

Richter closed in again and expended the rest of his 1029 rounds of ammunition, chopping off more of the aircraft's wing, smashing most of the instrument panel and injuring Hoang. In Richter's words, 'I saw my 20 mm rounds start to sparkle on his right wing the second time I fired. His right wing fell off. As I flew past I saw the MiG's canopy pop off'. Hoang ejected and Richter felt, 'happy that he got a good 'chute. He's a "jock" like I am, flying a plane, doing a job he has to do'.

As the F-105 pilots watched the MiG explode when it hit the ground, a second MiG-17 reappeared and attempted to move towards them, but Richter, out of ammunition and short of fuel, followed the leading 'Ford' element away from the area. At 23, he had become the youngest USAF pilot to score a MiG. Beardsley went on to complete his 100-mission tour.

CHAPTER THREE

'Vegas' flight from Takhli entered the area a few minutes later at 5000 ft, loaded with bombs. 'Vegas 1' saw a lone MiG-17 ahead of him making a right turn. He cut in the afterburner but retained his bombs as he accelerated behind the MiG and fired 154 rounds from a range of 2000 ft before his gun jammed. Some hits were observed on its wings, but as 'Vegas 1' thundered past him, jettisoning his stores and trying to recycle his gun, the MiG pilot also lit his afterburner, pulled up and rolled in behind the F-105. As a good wingman should, 1Lt Fred Wilson ('Vegas 2') moved in to protect his leader and fired 280 rounds from directly behind the MiG-17, seeing large chunks of its rear fuselage break away.

'He still had some fight in him and he could have fired at the leader', Wilson recalled. 'I just rushed up behind him firing my 20 mm gun all the time. My gunsight was not even set up. I just kept firing'. The MiG broke away in a dive to the left and Wilson saw an explosion on the ground that fitted its downward trajectory.

Moments later, 'Vegas 3' and '4' jettisoned their ordnance and went after a tan-camouflaged MiG-17, firing 135 rounds before 'Vegas 3's' gun jammed (probably because a burst-limiter had been incorrectly installed). They duly broke off the pursuit and headed home.

1Lt Karl Richter was shot down on 28 July 1967 flying F-105D 62-4334 *The Bat Bird*, assigned to Ed Rasimus. At a time when F-105 pilots had little more than a 50 per cent chance of completing a single combat tour, Richter came within hours of completing his second tour (*USAF*)

Opposite

1Lt Karl Richter (right) with 1Lt Fred A Wilson from Mobile, Alabama, who also destroyed a MiG-17 on 21 September 1966. Both kills occurred within about 35 miles of Hanoi, where pilots were particularly restricted by the Pentagon's frequently changing Rules of Engagement (RoE) that specified where, when and how MiGs could be attacked. Pilots were tested on the RoE weekly, and had to score 100 per cent. The restrictions included a ban on the delivery of ordnance in South Vietnam by Thailand-based aircraft. During a typical 2.5-hours mission a MiG engagement might occupy only a couple of minutes (*USAF*)

The big 650-gallon centreline and 450-gallon wing tanks could cause airframe damage if they were jettisoned at the wrong speed or attitude. F-105F 62-4420 'Tico 1' and its crew were apparently lost on 29 January 1967 when a wing tank knocked off its horizontal stabiliser. Some aircraft were damaged by the massive 650-gallon 'bag' when it reared up and struck the belly, rather than falling away (*via Peter Schinkelshoek*)

MiG-21s INTO BATTLE

There were three other engagements during the heavy Dap Cau attacks on 21 September – the third day of assaults on this rail and highway bridge. One of them almost resulted in a MiG-21 kill on a day when North Vietnamese GCI controllers began to vector the VPAF's most potent fighter into firing positions against US aircraft.

A 355th TFW flak suppression flight, leading five F-105 flights to the target, sighted four MiG-17s flying a parallel track to theirs. Shortly thereafter two MiG-21s dived at them from above. As the 'jettison ordnance' order was issued, a MiG-21 passed 1500 ft in front of the third F-105 in an attempt to attack the lead aircraft. The 'Thud' pilot fired but missed, and the MiG-21 pulled up in a half-chandelle and then chased the F-105, firing at it as the USAF jet dived for the deck. The MiG's wingman appeared in front of the fourth F-105, which fired a short burst at it and the pilot saw hits on the aircraft's belly before his gun stopped working. The MiGs vanished into the haze and no kill could be claimed.

A later strike flight dumped ordnance when MiG-17s approached, and one pilot had to perform a rapid manoeuvre to avoid the tumbling 650-gallon fuel tank from the aircraft ahead of him. The fourth pilot got separated from the flight when a MiG-17 briefly closed on his tail, firing at him. As he shook off the enemy fighter he saw another MiG-17 ahead of him, and fired 300 rounds at it, causing sparkling explosions all over the jet as it dived away.

The last F-105 strike flight on that unusually busy day also had a MiG kill opportunity. Reduced to two aircraft by technical aborts, the 388th TFW F-105s were jumped from behind by four MiG-17s. Having jettisoned their 3000 lbs of bombs, the 'Thud' pilots turned into their attackers and forced the MiGs to overshoot, although they killed their own speed as they reversed course. The lead F-105 pilot did not have time to re-set his gunsight and the MiGs roared past in afterburner – they were soon out of range after an encounter lasting less than a minute.

VPAF pilots did not strike again until 8 October when they engaged several incoming Thunderchief flights near Phuc Yen air base. On this mission the F-105s conducted a final, successful test of the QRC-160 ECM (electronic countermeasures) pod, which had been introduced in September under Project *Vampyrus* to protect Thunderchiefs from SAMs. Several MiG-17s were seen orbiting the runway at Phuc Yen, and the first flight of F-105s was attacked head-on as it left the target. Two more communist fighters also closed on the USAF jets from the rear, just missing one F-105 before the US fighters escaped in afterburner.

The flak suppression flight was also attacked just after it had laid its CBU-24 canisters on AAA sites, this time by four MiG-21s. Cleaning off their drop tanks and MERs, the F-105s pulled away as the MiGs used their well-tried tactic of trying to bring down the flight leader. His wingman was able to turn in behind a MiG-21, and he was convinced that he had hit it (his gun camera did not work) with some of the 235 bullets that he fired. Nevertheless, he did force the MiG to break off, despite having no gunsight. At that moment the flight leader's engine flamed out after it was struck by AAA, and his wingman had to abandon a likely MiG-21 kill to assist him. An air-start was made below 10,000 ft, this procedure being complicated by a SAM fired at the lead F-105 as he struggled to restore engine power. The missile was possibly diverted by the F-105's QRC-160 pod, which pilots generally welcomed despite its extra drag and perceived unreliability at high speed and low altitude.

The last F-105 flight to attack and leave the Phuc Yen target was intercepted twice by MiG-17s, which broke off on both occasions when the Thunderchief pilots outdistanced them in afterburner – they certainly earned their $2.16 a day combat bonus by bringing their aircraft home intact.

MiGs were sighted occasionally during the rest of October 1966, and their appearances increased in the second part of November as the use of QRC-160 pods became more widespread. The latter had reduced the SAM risk for F-105 crews from a level where losses to the missiles were becoming unsustainable. Indeed, only one pod-carrying F-105 was hit by a SAM between mid-October and December 1966. Flying in tighter 'pod' formations also reduced the strikers' time over the target, although it restricted the formation to shallow banking turns of 15 to 20 degrees to preserve the combined blanket downward coverage of the jamming pods'

Use of the AN/ALQ-71 (QRC-160A) ECM pod (seen here on the outer underwing pylon of F-105D 61-0198 of the 357th TFS in 1966) required F-105s to maintain close formation to maximise the jamming effect of their pods for optimum protection against the 'Fan Song' guidance radar for SA-2 'Dvina' SAMs and AAA fire-control radars. Revised AN/ALQ-87 (QRC-160-8) pods were introduced from late 1967 (*via Peter Schinkelshoek***)**

radiation. The 355th TFW generally favoured looser pod formations than the 388th TFW, with up to a mile separation between flights.

MiGs did not attempt to engage and take advantage of the F-105s' more restricted manoeuvrability until late November, when it soon became clear that revised tactics were being tried. VPAF ground controllers often vectored fighters beneath strike formations, masking their approach from American pilots by thin layers of cloud between them and the MiGs. At an appropriate point ground controllers would then command a 'pop-up' to place them behind and below the F-105s' 'blind spot'. Often, three MiGs would fly in trail formation so that if the F-105s saw the lead fighter and turned to avoid it, the USAF jets would fall within the field of fire of the second and third MiGs one mile behind.

December brought renewed MiG aggressiveness, which resulted in the final F-105 kill of the year. F-4 units had suffered heavy losses to SAMs because they did not have the F-105s' ECM pod protection (only 50 units were available at the time), and this in turn meant that MiGCAP escort flights were not allowed to enter the heavy SAM belts around Hanoi. With the Thunderchiefs left to go it alone against the defences, they duly attracted the MiGs' full attention. There was a dramatic increase in the number of aerial engagements, with almost 90 per cent of the MiG encounters in December involving attacks on F-105s, many of which were resisted aggressively. Keeping to effective 'pod' formation for optimum SAM protection meant flying relatively close together, minimising the chances of manoeuvring slightly to check the rear view.

The persistent difficulties with the F-105's armament switches probably lost another MiG-21 kill opportunity on 2 December, when two VPAF jets approached a Takhli strike flight as it completed delivery of its M117 bombs on a POL target at the end of 'Thud Ridge'. As they launched an attack on the second F-105 with two 'Atoll' missiles, the second F-105 element leader, who was trailing behind the lead pair, called for the No 2 jet to break as the missiles accelerated away from the MiGs. The weapons failed to guide, however, having probably been diverted by the low cloud and proximity to hilly terrain. One of the enemy fighters ended up in a vulnerable position only 200 ft abreast of the third Thunderchief, whose pilot was struggling to set up armament switches and could only head the MiG off by flying at him. The fourth F-105 pilot claimed that he could have had a good AIM-9 shot at the MiG as it broke away, but he was not carrying Sidewinders.

Two more MiG-21s attempted an interception minutes later as the strike force headed out along 'Thud Ridge'. The ever-vigilant second element leader called, 'We have two more coming up on us – push it up'. The F-105 pilots increased speed to around 650 knots and out-ran their pursuers. A single MiG-21 lined up on a later F-105 strike flight that

The kill marking on 62-4301 actually related to a claim for a VPAF Il-28 'Beagle' as a 'ground-kill'. During its nine years of active duty in the Far East this aircraft deployed to Takhli only briefly in 1966 (*Author's collection*)

day but it was seen off when the flight leader, a former B-52 pilot, called for a hard turn towards it.

An F-105 flight on an armed reconnaissance mission the following day was surprised to be intercepted by two MiG-21s over Route Pack V, almost 100 miles from Hanoi and well outside their normal area of activity. They turned away once they saw the Thunderchief flight dump its ordnance and head their way. Single MiG-21s followed F-105 flights several times in early December without engaging, and it was assumed that they were on training flights. However, the MiG-17s appeared in numbers to meet another POL strike near Phuc Yen on Sunday, 4 December, resulting in one of the biggest dogfights of the war and another MiG kill for the 388th TFW.

The first flight ('Detroit') of 355th TFW F-105Ds, including two un-camouflaged aircraft, on that late afternoon Phuc Yen POL raid rolled in to deliver its 750-lb bombs. As the leader, Capt Gerald 'Hawk' Hawkins, began his dive through heavy flak, he noticed no fewer than 16 silver MiG-17s in flights of four approaching from his right side at 7000 ft. Maj Ken Bell rolled 'wings level' to begin his attack and glanced across to his right, expecting to see his element leader, Lt Col Ben Murph (an ex-F-102A pilot who later took over the 474th TFW *Combat Lancer* F-111A detachment), but instead he saw a silver MiG-17 flying close formation off his wingtip. He lost the jet in the dive, but saw several others below him flying over the AAA site that his bombs were about to hit.

After pulling up from his bomb run Capt Hawkins made a somewhat vague transmission to 'get the MiGs' and promptly headed west to take on the armada, while the rest of his flight duly completed their bombing and prepared to exit the target area. Hawkins later commented;

'I was confident of my airplane, my equipment and myself. Frankly, with the frame of mind I was in if I ever got the chance I was definitely going to have a MiG. I just flat wanted to mix it up with a MiG.'

With 4000 hours of flight time and 800 hours on F-105s, Hawkins' self-assurance was understandable. He approached the suspected 'turkey shoot' from above, singling out a MiG-17 in the second flight and firing at it from a distance of 1500 ft down to 200 ft. Watkins had previously cleaned up his pylons (except for the precious QRC-160 pod) and set his fire control system to 'guns-air', but his gunsight would not hold a radar lock-on.

The VPAF pilot turned sharply away and another flight of MiGs began to achieve a firing position on Hawkins' F-105. This prompted the 'Thud' pilot to use a combination of ailerons and hard right rudder to make them overshoot. At 500 knots, with heavy AAA all around him, he deduced that the other MiG flights had too much mutual cover to make an attack profitable, but he saw a single MiG approaching head-on and dived towards it, opening fire from a distance of 2000 ft until he could tell that the bullets were passing behind his target. As the MiG fired back ineffectually, up to 25 20 mm hits became visible at one-foot intervals along its fuselage, and Hawkins saw pieces coming off the aircraft. Before the Thunderchief pilot could ascertain its fate he was distracted from his prey by 'little white cannon balls' passing close to his cockpit – he was under attack by two MiG-17PFs. Hawkins dropped to tree-top altitude at Mach 1.15 to outdistance the MiGs, which fired at him all the way, sending 'cannon balls' past his canopy.

Working in the F-105 'office' started with a long climb up the crew ladder, often at very unsociable hours. Maj Jack Spillers' F-105D 61-0220 stands ready for an early morning takeoff loaded with M118 'bridge-buster' bombs. North Vietnam's vital road and rail bridge targets were often the most likely places to encounter MiGs (*Jack Spillers via Norman Taylor*)

The other members of his flight, who might have been able to witness a kill (or possibly two) for him, were unaware of the exact motives for Hawkins' sudden departure until they received calls from him to the effect that he was swamped by MiGs and thought he had been hit. Lt Col Murph ordered them to return to the target area as he too turned back, but his message was apparently not received and the remaining two pilots continued to their exit point on the coast. Capt Ron Scott ('Detroit 2') almost exhausted his fuel trying to outrun another 'MiG', which was actually Maj Bell attempting to catch up with him. In fact, Bell thought he was catching up on Murph, who had been involved in a confusing radio exchange that suggested he wanted the flight to exit to the southwest as planned. Both were down to less than 800 lbs when they reached the tanker.

Meanwhile, Hawkins and then Murph made separate exits. Hawkins' engine flamed out as they crossed the Laotian border, but he got it re-started, and Murph's F-105 lost all its navigation gear. 'Detroit' flight returned to base, lucky to be alive.

The fourth flight on the same mission also encountered up to ten MiG-17s over the target area, possibly from the same formation, as they 'popped up' at 550 knots for their bomb runs. They were then intercepted by four more MiG-17s, which attacked from above and ahead. The second F-105 pilot in the flight, who was about to commence his dive, fired a 50-round eyeball-aimed snapshot as the VPAF jets crossed in front of the bombers, but the MiG he had targeted quickly reversed behind him. Moments later the No 3 F-105 pilot was able to get off 100 rounds in a 90-degree deflection shot at his counterpart in the MiG flight, using his windscreen for a gunsight, as his speed wound down to 300 knots in the tight turn.

Before he had to break off his attack on the MiG, the No 3 'Thud' pilot spotted an 'Atoll' heading for another F-105 as the flight attempted to rejoin for egress. By then it had become a 'daisy chain' of alternating MiGs and F-105s pursuing each other in trail, led by the F-105 flight leader, and firing guns or 'Atoll' missiles when possible. Fortunately, 'Atolls' were less accurate than the AIM-9Bs from which they were copied.

The Takhli aircraft had all been in constant afterburner throughout this fight and fuel was now getting short.

The other two POL-attacking Thunderchief flights that day also met MiG-17 opposition, and one pilot got in a good burst at an enemy fighter from a distance of only 800 ft in retaliation for some 23 mm gunfire aimed at him, but both missed. Once again, over-complex gunsight procedures on the US side were evident, and some of the 'new guy' pilots were also voicing concerns about their lack of training for aerial combat. Indeed, after action reports included comments that the five ACM flights provided by the Replacement Training Unit (RTU) at McConnell AFB were inadequate.

However, 4 December's many tangles with MiGs did in fact produce a kill when a large force of 40 F-105s was sent to the second target of the day – a railway yard north of Hanoi. The first wave of four flights abandoned the mission because of bad weather near the target, but the rest pressed on, noting two MiGs over Phuc Yen and two patrolling near the target. They did not approach the first flight of F-105s, but the second, 'Elgin' flight, saw several in the area as it approached the target. Pilots were duly jumped by four MiG-17s as they successfully completed their bombing runs.

Maj Roy S Dickey ('Elgin 04') saw a MiG-17 attacking his element leader, Capt Clint Murphy. The latter, in turn, detected two MiG-17s that had been lurking below the flak 'umbrella' as they closed in behind the flight leader, Capt Ray Bryant, and his wingman Capt McMahon, who were accelerating out at 600 knots. The flight also had to cope with very heavy AAA bursting around the F-105s. 'Elgin 03' (Murphy) set his fire control system to 'missiles-air' with radar search and attack (giving him a 1500 ft fixed range gunsight for his Vulcan cannon) and moved into a favourable firing position behind the enemy jets, unaware that he had another silver MiG-17 4000 ft behind him firing away. At that moment 'Elgin' lead was hit in the wing and horizontal tail by 37 mm AAA and 'Elgin 03' accelerated past the MiGs to escort his leader out of danger.

As last man off the target, Maj Dickey, on only his fourth mission over North Vietnam, fired 100 rounds into a warehouse as he pulled out of his dive-bombing attack. Looking into the sun to his left, he made out the outline of a MiG attacking 'Elgin 03'. With his gunsight still at the 122-mil bombing setting, Dickey estimated a lead angle on the MiG and began firing a continuous burst of 670 rounds, kicking his rudder to spread the fire and following the MiG into a 3g turn. It was only at this point that the pilot (probably 25-year-old Lt Luu Duc Si) of the communist jet became aware of the gunfire. Gun camera film showed more than 35 hits on the MiG, and flames began to emerge from its wing-root. When Dickey ceased firing at a range of 700 ft the entire fuselage behind the cockpit was wreathed in fire.

As the MiG entered a flat spin at 3500 ft Dickey spotted bullets passing his F-105 – the fourth MiG-17 pilot had closed in behind him and was now targeting the Thunderchief with all three guns. He jettisoned his wing tanks and bomb rack and dived to 50 ft, escaping at more than 600 knots with low fuel levels. Dickey suspected that the fourth MiG might have collided with his wing tanks as he jettisoned them. It was a quite a performance for an aircraft which, in F-105 pilot Hal Bingaman's words, was 'not really an air-to-air fighter'.

Maj Roy S Dickey, from Ashland, Kansas, at the conclusion of his 100th mission over North Vietnam. He claimed a MiG-17 kill on 4 December 1966 (*USAF*)

F-105D 60-0518, seen here in December 1968, was probably Maj Roy Dickey's mount on 4 December 1966 when he shot down a MiG-17. Thunderchief pilots learned the hard way that allowing the MiG pilot to draw them into a slow, turning fight invited disaster. The best option was to fire at the MiG, keep the speed up and return for another shot. To VPAF pilots in 1966, according to the Russian Ministry of Defence, 'the two weak points of the F-105D were its great sluggishness and insufficient manoeuvrability. American pilots adhered to defensive tactics and tried to disengage from the battle as quickly as possible' (*USAF*)

MiG activity continued at a high level throughout the first half of December 1966, with almost 90 per cent of the aerial engagements involving F-105 crews. A Takhli *Iron Hand* flight was engaged by a MiG-21 on 5 December, but its 'Atoll' missile was diverted earthward by ground heat when fired at an altitude of around 4000 ft. Another *Iron Hand* flight from Korat was not so lucky, however, losing Maj Burris Begley in F-105D 62-4331. The flight had received a MiG warning about a minute before two MiG-17s jumped it, but like many such radio calls it was not sufficiently specific about the exact location of the threat.

After Begley's aircraft was hit in its rear fuselage, releasing the brake parachute and pulling off large pieces of structure, his element leader moved in behind the MiGs to retaliate. He lined up for a clear shot and pulled the trigger repeatedly, but a broken gun-control box prevented the weapon from firing. Normally, pilots had been used to firing a quick burst into the air soon after takeoff to test and clear their guns, but this practice had been abandoned after several malfunctions had occurred following the test burst. A further MiG kill opportunity was thereby lost, and Begley was killed when his aircraft crashed minutes later.

The unreliability of the 'Atoll' missile, or lack of VPAF expertise, probably saved F-105 casualties on 8 December when three were fired from a group of eight MiG-21s closing behind two Thunderchief flights, led by Col Broughton. The mission was another re-attack on target JCS (Joint Chiefs of Staff) 19.00 – the POL and railway yard facilities near Phuc Yen (in the MiGs' backyard) – but heavy overcast prevented the strike on both primary and secondary targets. Two MiG-21s were vectored up through the cloud-base for coordinated attacks on mission commander Col Broughton's 'Kingpin' flight, while two more went for the second flight. All three missiles either exploded short or missed.

Both flights jettisoned their tanks but hung onto their bombs as long as possible as the MiGs continually tried for further attacks, but the ordnance eventually had to go and the enemy fighters then gave up the chase. However, a single grey-camouflaged MiG-21, allegedly flown by one of the VPAF's Soviet advisors, Snr Lt Vadim Shchbakov, passed 'Kingpin 1' at high speed in pursuit of 'Kingpin 3', who had flown ahead of Col Broughton and had a 'hung' wing tank. Whether the MiG, or possibly the heavy 37 mm AAA, shot down 'Kingpin 3' at low altitude or whether he hit the ground in the effort to avoid the MiG was never clear, but the lost pilot was the popular and highly capable Lt Col Don Asire, commander of the 354th TFS. His F-105D (59-1725) may have been the first to be shot down by a MiG-21. His replacement, Lt Col Gene Conley, was also shot down and killed (by AAA) a few weeks later.

1966 ended with large-scale aerial battles on 13, 14 and 19 December that resulted in one definite F-105 loss to a MiG-21's missile but no further MiG kills. On the 13th a 20-strong Thunderchief force was attacked by at least 15 MiG-17s and MiG-21s that were seen to be coordinating their activities with the SAM batteries that accounted for an F-105D and its 421st TFS pilot, Capt Sam Waters. The MiGs harassed the US formation with repeated missile and gun attacks, but never gave the F-105 pilots the opportunity to engage them.

The second Takhli flight to arrive over the Yen Vien railway yard target was met by 12 MiG-17s and MiG-21s. Brown smoke trails from six MiG-17s were seen ahead of the lead F-105 flight, which attempted to catch up with them, but the MiGs separated and vanished when the F-105 pilots approached gun range. They then tried to engage another four MiG-17s as they left the target but they too broke away. A third attempted attack on four 'bogies' was abandoned when they proved to be US Navy F-8 Crusaders and a fourth encounter was with two MiG-21PFs lying in wait as the Thunderchiefs headed home in the shelter of 'Thud Ridge'. No shots were fired by either side during any of these incidents, although the F-105 pilots felt that they might have achieved at least one kill had their jets been carrying Sidewinders.

Capt R B 'Spade' Cooley's aircraft (60-0502) was hit on 14 December – a day when 175 US sorties were flown over North Vietnam – by an 'Atoll' from Dong Van De's MiG-21PF (4212), the VPAF pilot having dived from 6000 ft onto a formation of 40 F-105s. The missile, fired from behind Cooley's jet, caused the Thunderchief's engine to explode and his aircraft to disintegrate around him. 60-0502 was officially the first US loss to an air-to-air missile. Cooley ejected with a fractured spine, and he was eventually snatched from imminent capture in one of the deepest penetrations into North Vietnam by an HH-3 rescue helicopter and its A-1 Skyraider escorts.

Six MiGs attacked the Thunderchief flights that day and only one pilot had a chance to retaliate, firing without a gunsight at close range but without visible hits. Two *Iron Hand* pilots had the frustrating experience of watching a pair of MiG-21s pass above them, flying in their direction and unaware of their presence. The MiGs were in ideal Sidewinder range for the 'Thud' pilots, who were unable to catch them up because of their own heavy ordnance loads, which did not include AIM-9Bs.

F-105 flights revisiting the target on 19 December met 18 VPAF fighters, and the pilots involved thought that they had identified single 'tutor' MiG instructors flying some distance from the main formations and relaying instructions to them. Other than forcing three of the five flights to dump their ordnance, the MiGs had no gains or losses that day. Several F-105 pilots who had not seen MiGs previously were amazed at their turning performance and, once again, were frustrated by the labour-intensive procedures for setting up their armament for air-to-air while simultaneously selecting ordnance items to jettison. Usually, by the time all of this had been completed, the MiGs had already departed.

COLOUR PLATES

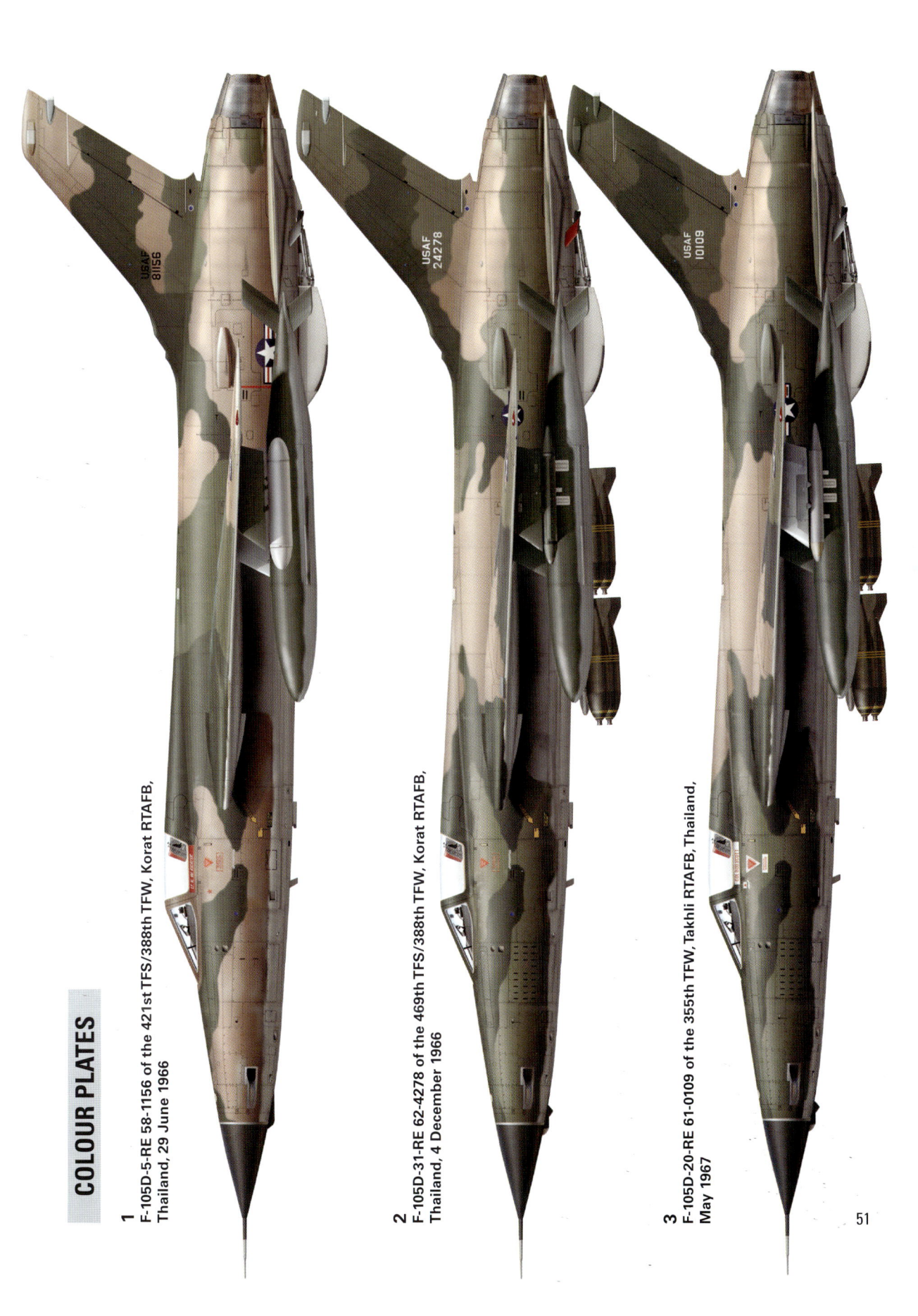

1
F-105D-5-RE 58-1156 of the 421st TFS/388th TFW, Korat RTAFB, Thailand, 29 June 1966

2
F-105D-31-RE 62-4278 of the 469th TFS/388th TFW, Korat RTAFB, Thailand, 4 December 1966

3
F-105D-20-RE 61-0109 of the 355th TFW, Takhli RTAFB, Thailand, May 1967

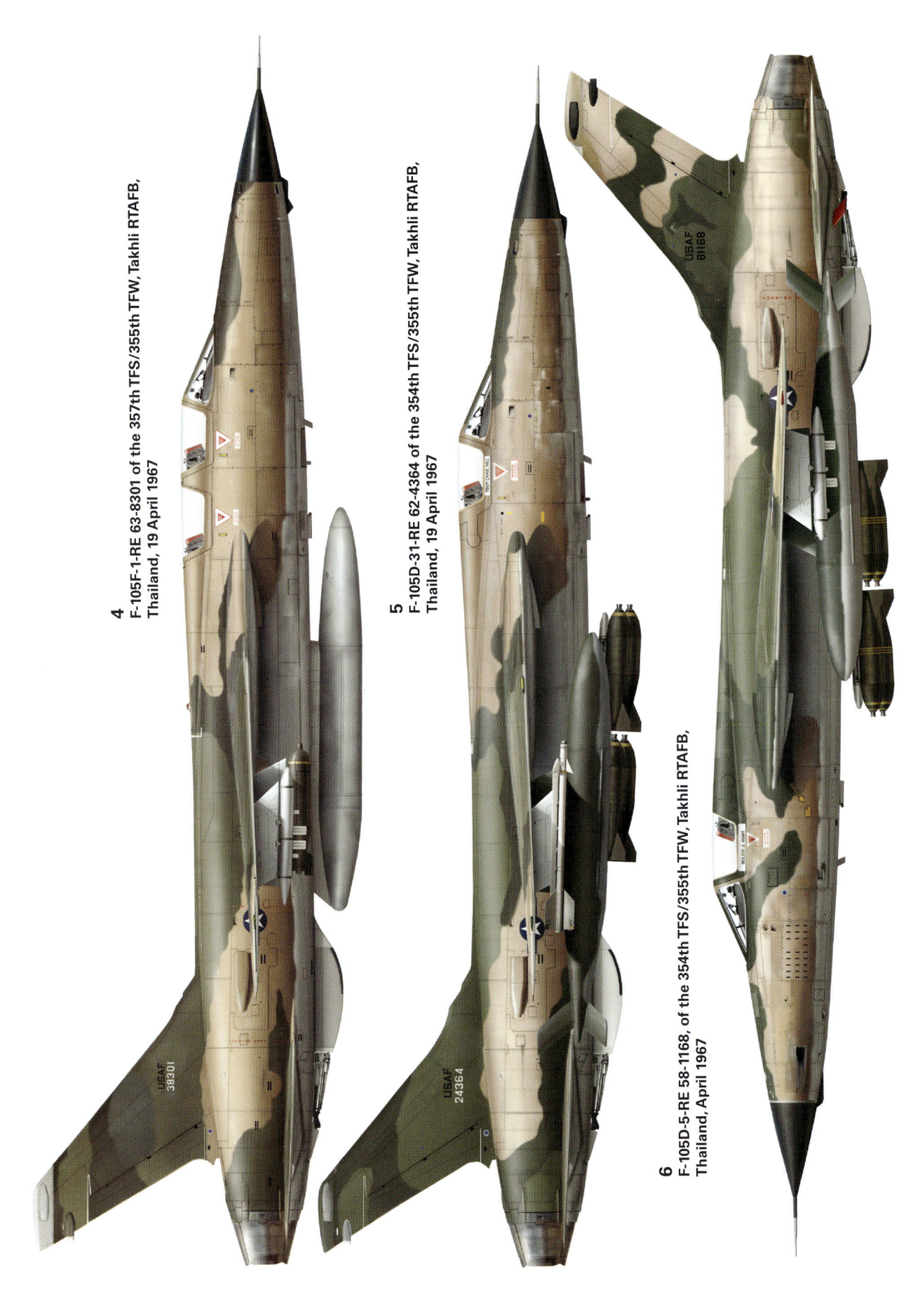

4
F-105F-1-RE 63-8301 of the 357th TFS/355th TFW, Takhli RTAFB, Thailand, 19 April 1967

5
F-105D-31-RE 62-4364 of the 354th TFS/355th TFW, Takhli RTAFB, Thailand, 19 April 1967

6
F-105D-5-RE 58-1168, of the 354th TFS/355th TFW, Takhli RTAFB, Thailand, April 1967

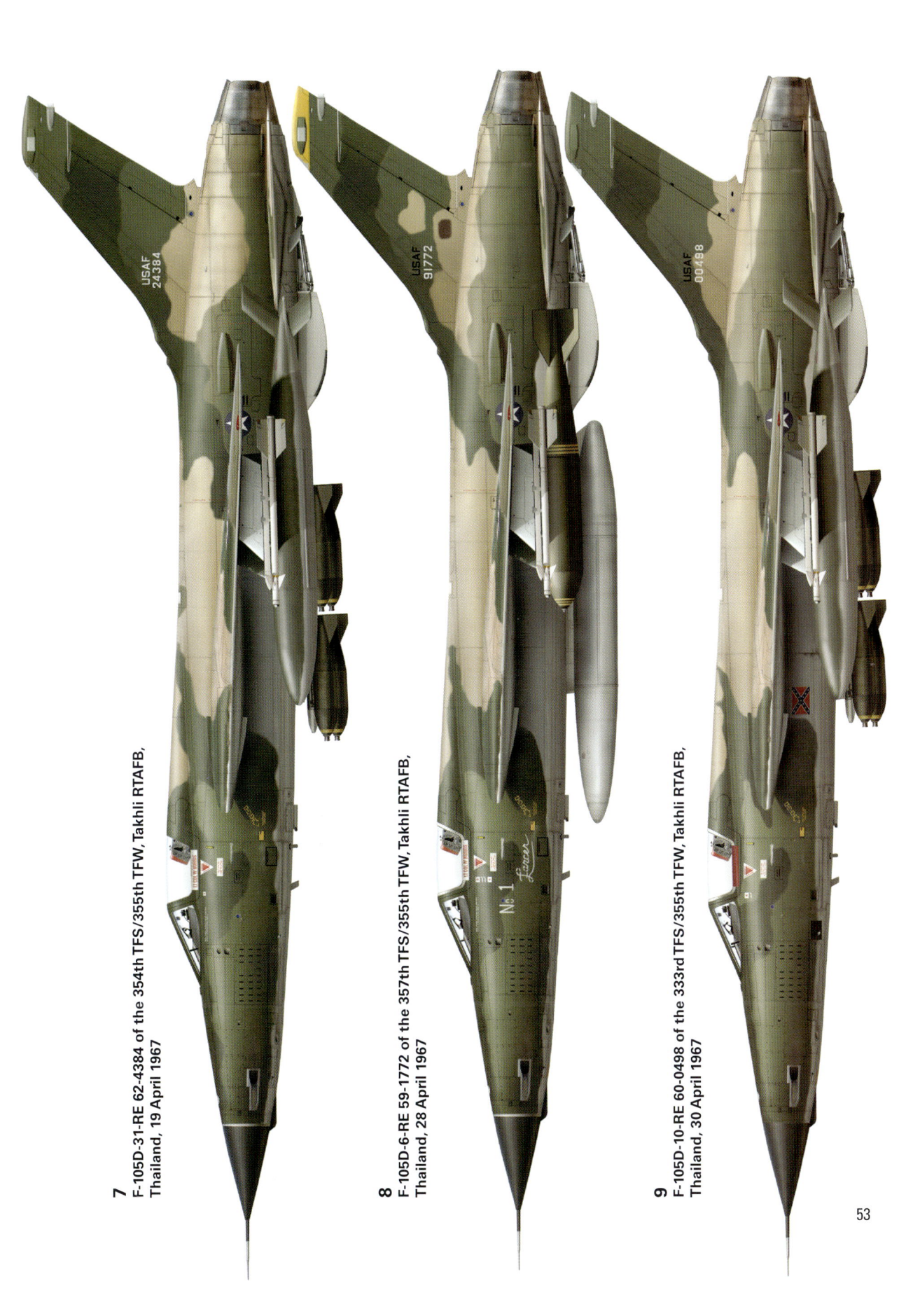

7
F-105D-31-RE 62-4384 of the 354th TFS/355th TFW, Takhli RTAFB, Thailand, 19 April 1967

8
F-105D-6-RE 59-1772 of the 357th TFS/355th TFW, Takhli RTAFB, Thailand, 28 April 1967

9
F-105D-10-RE 60-0498 of the 333rd TFS/355th TFW, Takhli RTAFB, Thailand, 30 April 1967

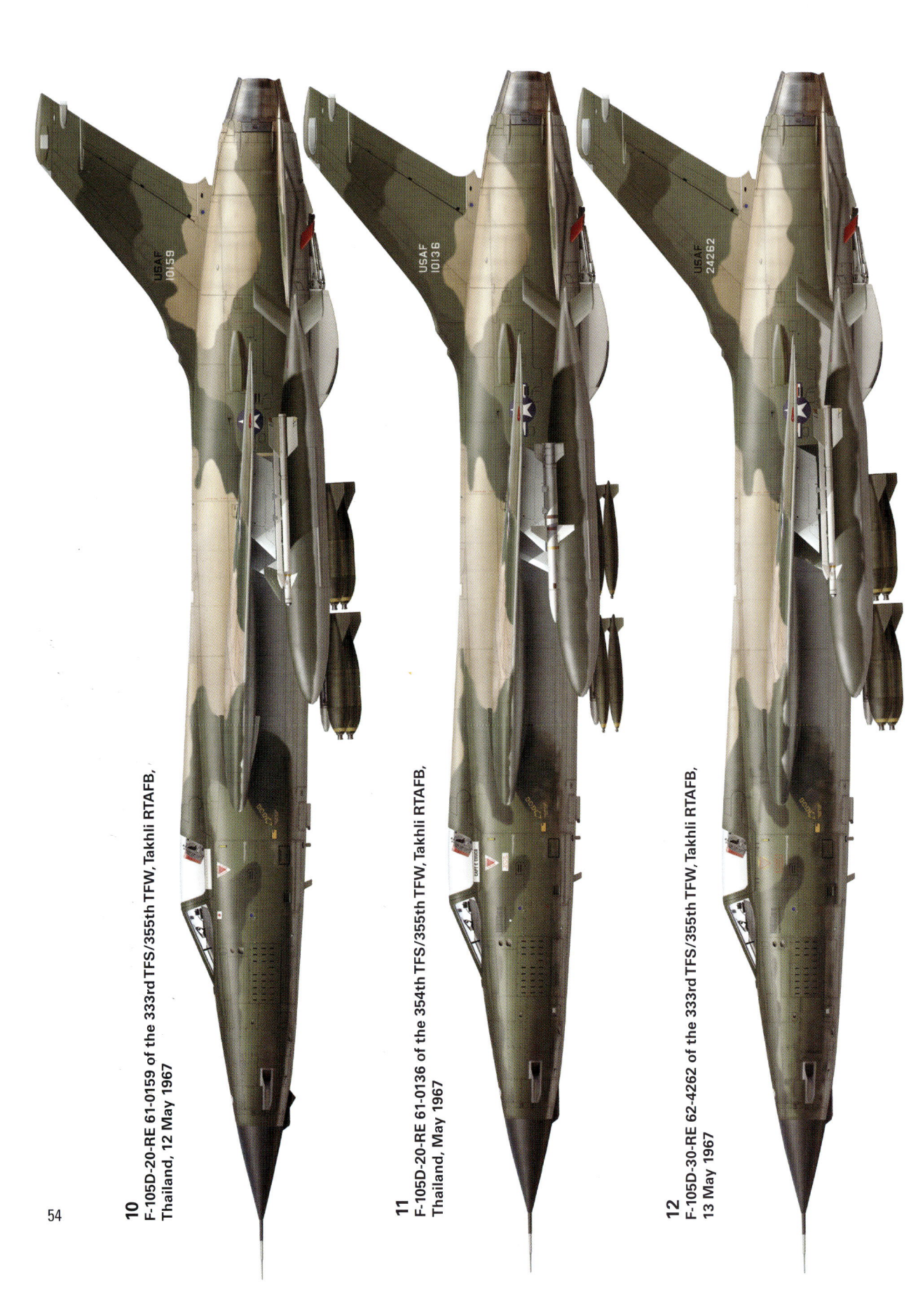

10
F-105D-20-RE 61-0159 of the 333rd TFS/355th TFW, Takhli RTAFB,
Thailand, 12 May 1967

11
F-105D-20-RE 61-0136 of the 354th TFS/355th TFW, Takhli RTAFB,
Thailand, May 1967

12
F-105D-30-RE 62-4262 of the 333rd TFS/355th TFW, Takhli RTAFB,
13 May 1967

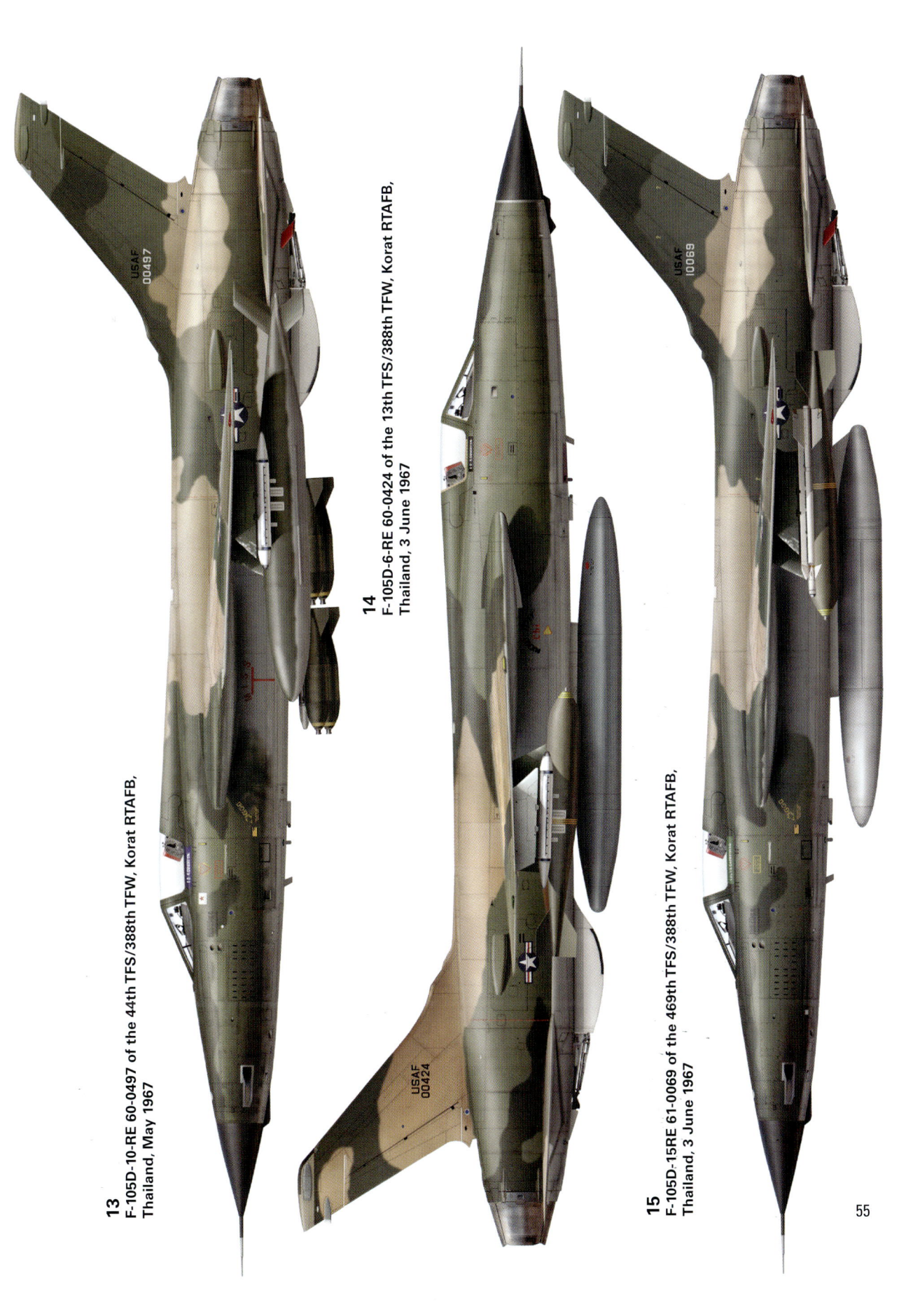

13
F-105D-10-RE 60-0497 of the 44th TFS/388th TFW, Korat RTAFB, Thailand, May 1967

14
F-105D-6-RE 60-0424 of the 13th TFS/388th TFW, Korat RTAFB, Thailand, 3 June 1967

15
F-105D-15RE 61-0069 of the 469th TFS/388th TFW, Korat RTAFB, Thailand, 3 June 1967

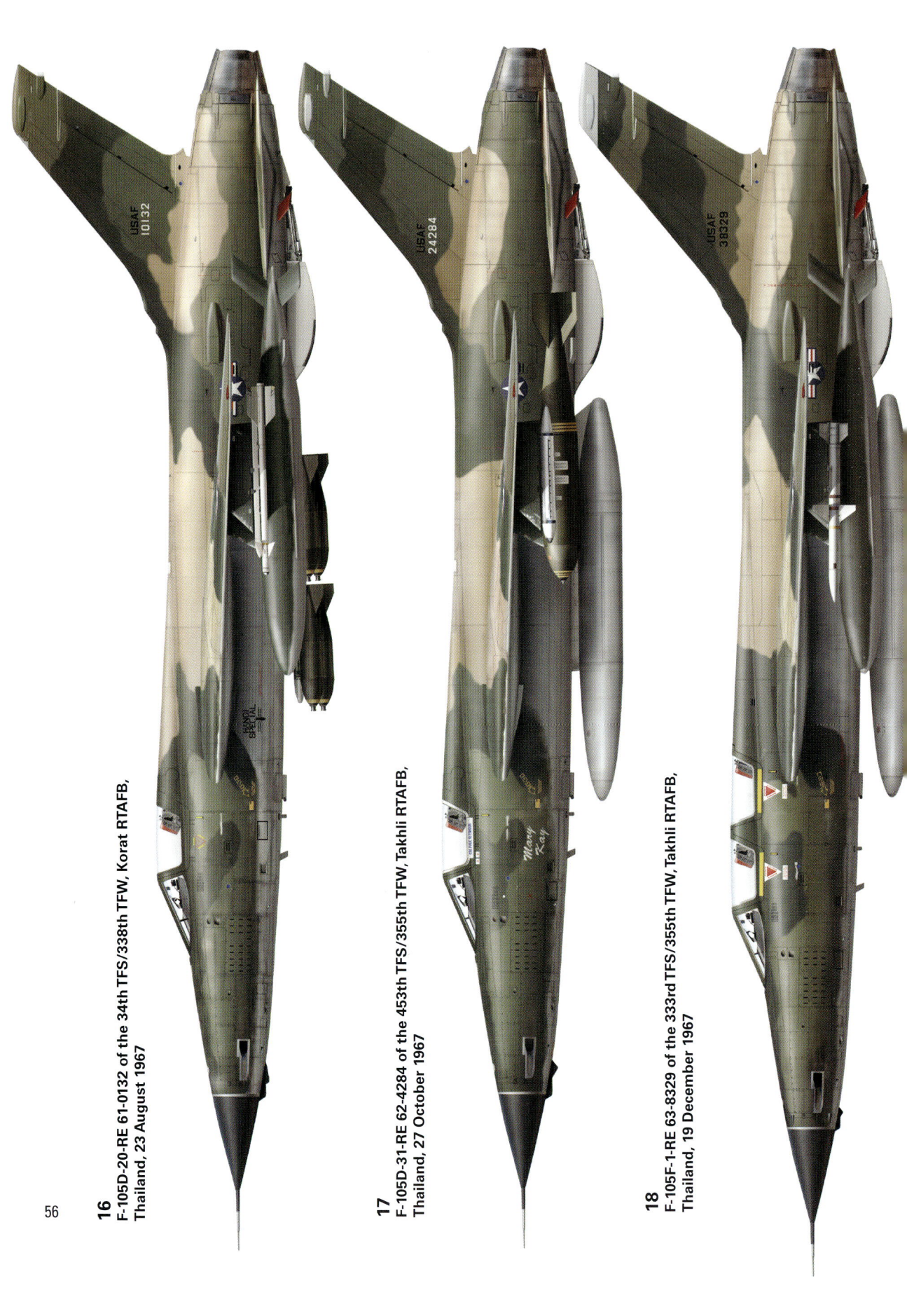

16
F-105D-20-RE 61-0132 of the 34th TFS/338th TFW, Korat RTAFB, Thailand, 23 August 1967

17
F-105D-31-RE 62-4284 of the 453rd TFS/355th TFW, Takhli RTAFB, Thailand, 27 October 1967

18
F-105F-1-RE 63-8329 of the 333rd TFS/355th TFW, Takhli RTAFB, Thailand, 19 December 1967

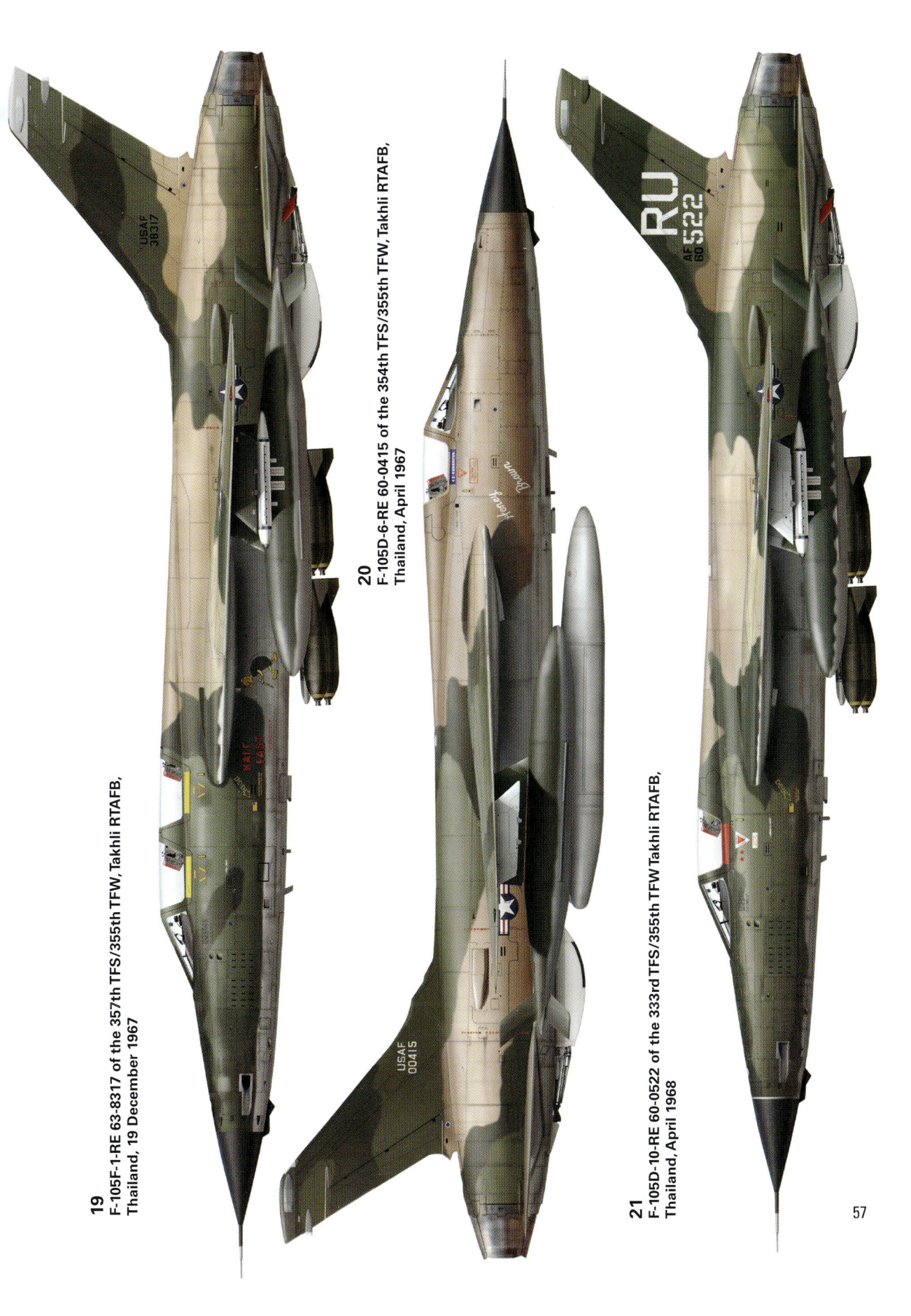

19
F-105F-1-RE 63-8317 of the 357th TFS/355th TFW, Takhli RTAFB,
Thailand, 19 December 1967

20
F-105D-6-RE 60-0415 of the 354th TFS/355th TFW, Takhli RTAFB,
Thailand, April 1967

21
F-105D-10-RE 60-0522 of the 333rd TFS/355th TFW Takhli RTAFB,
Thailand, April 1968

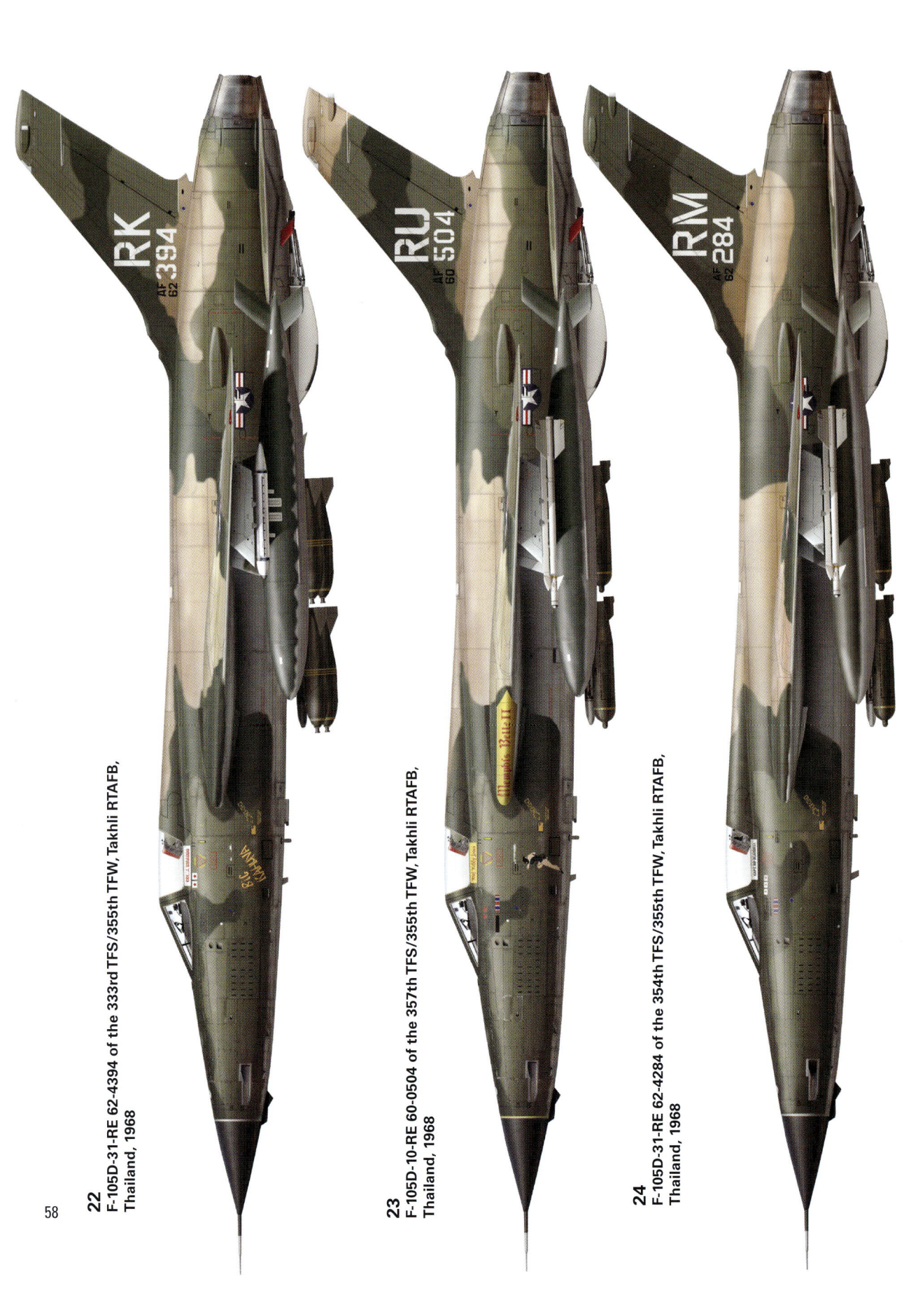

22
F-105D-31-RE 62-4394 of the 333rd TFS/355th TFW, Takhli RTAFB, Thailand, 1968

23
F-105D-10-RE 60-0504 of the 357th TFS/355th TFW, Takhli RTAFB, Thailand, 1968

24
F-105D-31-RE 62-4284 of the 354th TFS/355th TFW, Takhli RTAFB, Thailand, 1968

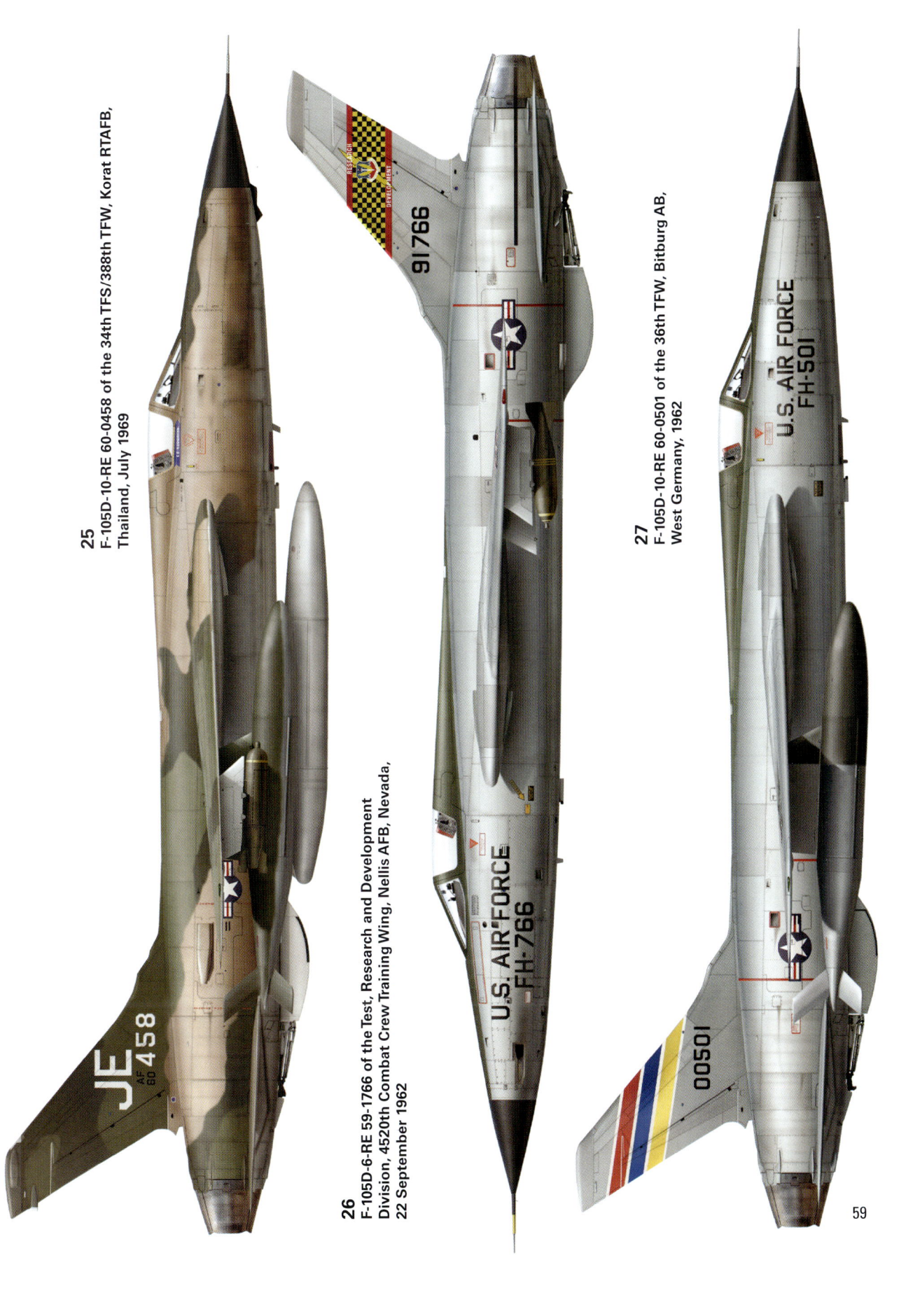

25
F-105D-10-RE 60-0458 of the 34th TFS/388th TFW, Korat RTAFB, Thailand, July 1969

26
F-105D-6-RE 59-1766 of the Test, Research and Development Division, 4520th Combat Crew Training Wing, Nellis AFB, Nevada, 22 September 1962

27
F-105D-10-RE 60-0501 of the 36th TFW, Bitburg AB, West Germany, 1962

28
F-105D-20-RE 61-0159 of the 149th TFS/192nd TFG, Virginia ANG, Byrd ANGB, Virginia, 1980

29
F-105D-15-RE 61-0069 of the 466th TFS/508th TFG, Hill AFB, Utah, 1981

30
F-105D-31-RE 62-4301 of the 466th TFS/419th TFW, Hill AFB, Utah, 1983

1967 – MiG MAYHEM

The high level of MiG activity at the end of 1966 and the loss of 19 US aircraft (including seven F-105s) to MiGs since April 1965 prompted an initiative within the 8th TFW at Ubon RTAFB that dealt the 921st FR MiG-21s a devastating blow. The latter unit's tactics had become particularly aggressive in December 1966, and more than one-fifth of US strike aircraft had been forced to jettison their ordnance loads during that month.

Using a plan conceived by the 8th TFW tactics officer, Capt John B Stone, and the CO, Col Robin Olds, F-4C Phantom IIs, simulating the call-signs, flight patterns and attack routes of the F-105 wings, flew close to the MiG base at Phuc Yen emitting jamming signals from QRC-160 (AN/ALQ-71) ECM pods hastily borrowed from Thunderchief units. A US Navy team had previously approached the 355th TFW with a similar plan, using F-105s as 'bait' for their F-8 Crusader fighters. For the 8th TFW's Operation *Bolo*, Takhli F-105s flew their usual *Iron Hand* sorties, sighting but not engaging MiG-21s. The MiGs rose to the bait and found Phantom IIs waiting for them above the dense overcast. Seven were shot down on 2 January 1967 (followed by two more in a similar 'sting' four days later) and the 921st FR effectively stood down for several weeks to revise tactics and re-train, having lost up to half of its operational MiG-21s.

Individual MiG-21s were occasionally seen flying parallel to strike formations, apparently observing them. Flights of MiG-21s approached F-105s several times during early January, but they broke away rather than engaging the USAF jets. On 16 January MiGs approached close enough to force F-105s to jettison ordnance, but generally they made distant, simulated approaches and withdrew if the F-105s turned towards them. Two flights of MiG-21s did make firing passes on Korat aircraft during the 21 January attack on Viet Tri railway yard, however, diving through the formation and forcing a 'jettison' order from the flight leader. Although the F-105s retained their Sidewinders, there was no chance to use them before the MiGs quickly vanished after what one Korat pilot described as a 'very aggressive attack'.

MiG-17s still comprised the bulk of the VPAF fighter force, and the 21 January interception was accompanied by fighters making firing passes on all four aircraft in a 355th TFW *Wild Weasel* flight ('Panda'). 'Panda 4' (Maj Ed Dobson), was hit in the wing by two 23 mm shells but was able to escape. 'Panda 2's' afterburner went out during a steep turn but, with speed

The 388th TFW in residence at Korat RTAFB in January 1967 (*Terry Panopalis collection***)**

reduced to 400 knots, he was still able to fire three bursts of 20 mm cannon rounds at a MiG-17 that was attacking the flight leader. Lacking a correctly adjusted gunsight, his purpose was mainly to scare the MiG away, but his gun jammed after the third burst and no hits were seen. At such slow speed he was immediately picked on by another of the five MiG-17s, and he descended to an altitude of less than 50 ft, watching the MiG's shells exploding on the ground ahead of him. A second MiG then took up the chase as the F-105's speed dropped to 350 knots, the 'Thud' pilot turning into each attack. This tactic allowed him to hold off the VPAF fighters until they eventually left, presumably out of ammunition.

Sidewinders had been fired by F-105Ds since at least 19 July 1966 when Capt David J Allinson (No 3 in 'Steel' flight, led by Maj Jim Kasler) expended two at MiG-17s. A 388th TFW flight, in which all four aircraft had AIM-9Bs, fired at a MiG on 22 January 1967 during a Thang Quang railway yard mission. The F-105D element leader targeted his Sidewinder at a MiG-17 that was firing at the flight leader. Although the missile emitted a good lock-on tone it was unable to follow the MiG when its pilot made a steep downwards turn. The MiGs headed for Hanoi and the F-105 flight chose not to follow them into the city's formidable SAM site belt.

Another Sidewinder was fired at a MiG-17 on 4 February, and it appeared to be homing successfully, but the MiG disappeared into haze and the results were unseen. No VPAF losses were recorded that day and its fighters avoided confrontation with US aircraft for the rest of that month.

THE GLORIOUS TENTH

From mid-February 1967 there was a concerted attempt to disrupt North Vietnam's transportation, airfields and industry with heavy, repeated air strikes. March brought an end to the northeast monsoon, which had impeded air activity throughout January and February, and MiG activity resumed during a series of attacks on the vast Thai Nguyen Iron and Steel Works complex (JCS 76.00) by 72 F-105s and F-4s. In all, six aircraft were lost and others received considerable AAA damage in two days of attacks on this heavily defended target.

The StrikeCAP F-4C Phantom IIs on the first 10 March mission saw off the opening MiG attack – a missile launch from a MiG-21 that stalked a departing F-105 flight and climbed from 3000 ft below their 'six o'clock'. Luckily, the 'Atoll' was fired too far away and the MiG broke off its attack when an F-4C fired an unguided Sparrow missile as a distraction.

The flak suppression flight ('Kangaroo') led by Lt Col Philip Gast (who had replaced Gene Conley as 354th TFS squadron commander and was flying as 355th TFW mission commander on this occasion) encountered MiG-21s as it approached the target. 'Kangaroo 3', the voluble Capt Max C Brestel of Takhli's 354th TFS, turned their way to distract them from attacking Lt Col Gast, before continuing his bomb run to drop four CBU-24 canisters. 'Kangaroo 2', unaware of the MiG-17s, withdrew with radio failure at this point. He also experienced a jammed gun when he attempted to fire at a MiG-21 as he exited. Minutes later he joined up with another F-105 that was attacking a SAM site.

Lt Gen Philip C Gast in March 1980. Born in 1930, he flew the RF-84F and F-101C Voodoo before joining the 355th TFW operations staff in July 1966. Gast completed 114 combat missions and shot down a MiG-17 on 13 May 1967, when F-105Ds destroyed five MiGs. In November 1967 he took over the 10th TFS at Hahn AB, in West Germany, flying F-4D Phantom IIs (*Joe Collaso/DAOP*)

Col Jacksel Broughton (left), vice wing commander of the 355th TFW, congratulates Capt Max C Brestel, the USAF's first Vietnam double MiG killer, after his 100th mission. Brestel had joined the 354th TFS as a flight leader on 4 November 1966. Col Broughton praised the F-105's ability to 'go like a dingbat on the deck' but criticised the USAF policy of ordering 'large supersonic flatirons' that should have had rearward-firing missiles, as 'that seems to be where the MiGs show up most of the time – on our behinds'. USAF planners considered that dogfighting ability and resistance to battle damage were irrelevant for a nuclear strike aircraft like the F-105 (*USAF*)

Brestel moved in to fill the gap left by 'Kangaroo 2'. Lt Col Gast then saw four MiG-17s about a mile ahead of them and transmitted, 'Let's go get them'. Brestel responded 'I'm with you' and then noticed another quartet of MiG-17s following 1500 ft behind the first flight. Gast, barrel-rolling and S-turning, attempted to fire an AIM-9B at them, but the complex switchology failed him. Capt Brestel had the same problem, and he also had no time in which to set up his gunsight as he was 'too busy with the speed brakes, afterburner and flaps'. He attempted to get an electrically caged sight but in the end just aimed along the top line of the gunsight's combining glass, pointing his Thunderchief 'in the general direction of the MiG'. Brestel later commented, 'everyone uses various methods to bugger the F-105 system'. Gast reverted to the gun and saw sparkles on the wing of a MiG-17 as his shells damaged it.

'I observed all MiGs light their afterburners', Brestel continued. 'Lt Col Gast began firing at one of the first two MiGs. I observed the second two beginning to fire at Gast. I called a break and closed to within 300-500 ft of the No 4 MiG. I fired an approximate 2.5-second burst, observing hits in the wing, fuselage and canopy and a fire in the left wing root. The aircraft rolled over and hit the ground under my left wing.' Gast transmitted, 'I got one! I got one!' and received the anonymous response, 'Shut your mouth and get another one!'

'I then closed to 300 ft on the No 3 MiG, which was firing at Lt Col Gast', Brestel continued. 'He was in a right turn, and again I fired a 2.5-second burst, observing more hits and pieces flying off the aircraft. The aircraft appeared to flip back over my canopy and disappeared behind me. We broke off the engagement at this time after approximately one-and-a-half to two minutes of combat. A SAM was fired at us, as was more flak, as we exited the area. I know I destroyed the first MiG as I saw him crash. My wingman, 1Lt Robert L Wescamp, also observed the MiG hit the ground. I feel I also destroyed the second MiG, as the range was the same and hits were observed in the same area. Also, his last manoeuvre could not be considered normal. The aircraft appeared to be in a violent pitch-up and out of control.'

Brestel was awarded both MiGs, making him the first USAF double MiG killer of the war. On the same day Capt Merlyn H Dethlefsen flew his 78th mission – one for which he was awarded the Medal of Honor. His 355th TFW *Iron Hand* 'Lincoln' flight had preceded the F-105 strike flights to the Thai Nguyen target, and as it attacked a SAM site 'Lincoln 1' (Maj David Everson and Capt Dave Luna) was shot down by a direct 85 mm flak hit in the nose area. Both crewmen were taken prisoner. Despite his F-105F being holed by AAA and a MiG shooting up the right wing of the F-105D flown by his wingman, Maj Ken Bell, Dethlefsen defeated two MiG-21s that were pursuing him by flying into an area of heavy flak bursts, which in turn forced the VPAF pilots to break off their pursuit. Capts Dethlefsen and Gilroy, with Maj Bell, then proceeded to attack a SAM site, destroying it in four passes with bombs and gunfire.

There were two other notable events in USAF history on 10 March. In the legendary F-4 recovery operation later dubbed 'Pardo's Push', two 8th TFW F-4C Phantom IIs of 'Cheetah' MiGCAP flight reached safe bail-out areas after Capt Bob Pardo placed his windscreen against the lowered tail-hook of Capt Earl Aman's fuel-starved jet and literally pushed it for ten minutes. It was also the day on which President Johnson publicly acknowledged that F-105 operations were being conducted from politically neutral Thailand. This had been an official secret, but few were surprised by the revelation. As Thunderchief pilot Capt Willard Snell quipped, 'No-one knew except the enemy'.

Col Robert Scott, commander of the 355th TFW, was the next to destroy a MiG-17. Leading 'Leech' strike flight of the 333rd TFS in 59-1772 on 26 March in the Hoa Lac area, he passed close to the local MiG base. Scott's account of the engagement demonstrated how the MiG-17's superior turning ability was not always sufficient defence against a skilful US pilot;

'I had acquired the target and executed a dive-bomb run. During the recovery I observed a MiG taking off from Hoa Lac airfield. I began a left turn to follow the MiG for possible engagement. At this time I observed three more MiG-17s orbiting the airfield at approximately 3000 ft in single-ship trail, with 3000 ft to 5000 ft spacing. The MiGs were silver with red stars. I then concentrated my attention on the nearest MiG-17 and pressed the attack. As I closed on the MiG it began a turn to the right. I followed the jet, turning inside, and began firing. I observed ordnance impacting on the left wing and pieces of material tearing off. At this time the MiG began a hard left descending turn. I began to overshoot and pulled off high and to the right. The last time I saw the MiG it was extremely low, at approximately 500 ft, and rolling nose down.'

Members of another F-105 flight saw a MiG-17 crash and VPAF records include the loss of Lt Vu Huy in that engagement.

Aircraft in the second 'Leech' element had an 'Atoll' fired at them by a MiG-21 as the jets left the target, and a camouflaged SAM rose towards

Col Robert R Scott took over F-105D 61-0109 and displayed his MiG kill on it, this marking having been transferred from his MiG-17 killer, 59-1772. Although Scott was replaced as 355th TFW commander by Col Jon C Giraudo on 2 August 1967, 61-0109 continued to serve as the CO's F-105D, being decorated with Giraudo's nickname, *Big Kahuna*. The right side of the nose bore the slogan *Surf's Up*. Maj Don Russell's MiG killer 62-4394 also wore the *Big Kahuna* nickname while assigned to the 333rd TFS (*Bob Archer collection*)

them seconds later. Both missiles passed uncomfortably close by. Three other F-105s were involved in brief gun battles with MiG-17s that day, but generally the MiGs chose to engage the F-4C StrikeCAP flight, with no results on either side.

From then until 19 April MiG sightings were sporadic, and both MiG-17 and MiG-21 pilots tended to break off potential engagements when F-105s turned towards them. One such situation occurred on 11 April when four strike F-105s saw three MiG-21s turning towards them. The Thunderchief flight leader turned head-on towards the MiGs, the two fighter formations now having a combined closing speed of around 1000 knots. The F-105s retained their bomb loads. At a range of seven miles the MiG leader broke off from this duel of nerves and took his flight home.

FOUR DOWN

For the 355th TFW, 19 April 1967 was a remarkable day during which four more MiGs were destroyed, a fifth was damaged and a second Medal of Honor was awarded to an F-105 *Iron Hand* pilot in some of the most strenuous aerial combat of the Vietnam War. However, the *Iron Hand* crews sustained their tenth loss on this particularly hazardous type of mission.

'Kingfish' flight from the 355th TFW was in the vanguard of the action on the 19th whilst performing the *Iron Hand* role for six flights of F-105s and F-4Cs striking the Xuan Mai army barracks complex north of Hanoi. Amongst the jets involved in the strike were four *Wild Weasel* F-105Fs, with the first element led by Maj Leo Thorsness and Capt Harry Johnson ('Kingfish 1') and the second element led by Majs Thomas Madison and Thomas Sterling ('Kingfish 2'). They split the flight experimentally so that four F-105Fs could attack two SAM sites at once.

Although a SAM site protecting the barracks was knocked out by the first element using Shrikes and CBU-24s, the second element was engaged head-on by four MiG-17s firing unguided rockets, forcing both F-105 crews to jettison ordnance. 'Kingfish 4' lost his afterburner and became a target for volleys of rockets and cannon shells. Nevertheless, the 'Thud' pilot managed to fire a short burst that probably damaged one of the VPAF aircraft. He eventually extricated himself with help from Jerry Hoblit and Tom Wilson in 'Kingfish 3', who distracted the MiGs long enough for the crippled jet to make a hazardous low-altitude exit in mountainous terrain without afterburner, pursued for several miles by MiG-17s that eventually turned back one by one.

During this low-altitude manoeuvring several of the ten MiG-17s seen during the engagement attempted to close in behind the *Wild Weasel* aircraft as they made their second run. Suddenly, Hoblit called '"Kingfish 2" is hit!' Madison and Sterling's F-105F (63-8341, used for Capt Dethlefsen's Medal of Honor mission) had been attacked by another MiG-17 as they and Maj Thorsness

355th TFW commander Col Robert R Scott (left) downed his MiG on 26 March 1967. On 13 July he was on hand to greet MiG killer Lt Col Arthur F Dennis at Tan Son Nhut AB after his 100th mission. Also present was surprise guest, and fellow Texan, film star Gene Autry, the singing cowboy (right). Dennis enlisted as an aircraft mechanic in 1948 and then applied for pilot training. He flew 100 combat missions in Korea (in F-80s and F-84s) and another 100 in the F-105, during which he was hit three times. He commented, 'The hardest part is waiting before a mission. We receive our mission assignments the night before and it's a job staying mentally and physically alert for any task. Once you are in the aircraft and on the way everything is fine' (*USAF*)

CHAPTER FOUR

headed for a second SAM site with CBU-24 canisters. Madison reported warning lights in his cockpit as he headed out, and he and Sterling had to eject seconds later. The following flight of F-105D strikers saw smoke coming from the aircraft as the MiG continued to shoot at it, while Leo Thorsness spotted 'Kingfish 2's' parachutes ahead of him. He also noticed a MiG-17 heading towards the parachutes, and calculated that the pilot was planning to strafe the *Wild Weasel* crew. He accelerated to 500 knots, diving at the MiG.

'I initially opened fire with 300 rounds from an estimated 2000-1500 ft in a right-hand shallow pursuit curve', Thorsness reported. 'No impacts were observed. Within a few seconds we were in the "six o'clock" position, with 75-100 knots of overtake speed. I fired another burst of 300 rounds with a caged sight reticle, then pulled up to avoid both the debris and the MiG. It was approximately 100 ft below us and to our left. Several rips were noted on the battered left wing. Capt Johnson sighted a MiG-17 at our "6.30" position approximately 2000 ft back. I pulled into a tighter turn, selected afterburner and lowered the nose. I again looked at the crippled MiG and saw it impact the ground in what appeared to be a rice field'. 'Kingfish Lead' then headed off to the foothills.

Having heard Maj Thorsness's call that the crew of 'Kingfish 2' had bailed out, 'Kingfish 4' returned to the target area in his crippled F-105 in order to provide a radio relay for the RESCAP effort until his fuel ran low. 'Kingfish 3' also attempted to return, but a succession of MiG-17s kept the jet away from the rescue site until it too had reached 'bingo' fuel. This meant that when the RESCAP effort for

Maj Leo K Thorsness and Capt Harold E Johnson pose for a USAF photographer. Their one aircraft, Medal of Honor war against ten MiGs in an attempt to rescue Majs Madison and Sterling on 19 April 1967 developed into one of the biggest aerial battles of the conflict for F-105 pilots, and resulted in four aerial victories for the 355th TFW. In Maj Thorsness' opinion, 'The F-105 was a very fast airplane that could not turn'. Australian bush hats were *de rigeur* for F-105 crews, being used to mark off missions flown (applied to the hats in red ink for Route Pack VI) and record progress towards the 'magic 100th' combat mission (*USAF*)

Opposite
Two *Wild Weasel*-modified F-105Fs en route to war, the nearest (63-8267) bound for the 357th TFS/355th TFW at Takhli RTAFB and the other (63-8272) heading for the 13th TFS/388th TFW at Korat. Their SAM-suppression missions, among the most hazardous of the conflict, attracted considerable attention from MiGs, leading to several MiG kills by escorting F-105Ds and by the F-105F crews themselves. The tough Thunderchief often survived SAM detonations. One took hits in 87 places by SA-2 fragments, which removed the ventral fin, the top of the fin and rudder and the engine gang drain. A major fuselage frame was broken and the pilot was wounded, but he managed to refuel from a KC-135A and return to base (*via Peter Schinkelshoek*)

Maj Jack W Hunt, known for his dry sense of humour, at the end of his 100th mission. His aircraft (58-1168 *Betty's Boy*) carries his MiG kill marking beneath the windscreen (*USAF*)

'Kingfish 2' got underway Thorsness's F-105, despite a shortage of fuel and almost expended ordnance, was the only one left in the area to guide in the rescue HH-3 helicopter and its A-1E 'Sandy' escort, and defend them from the MiGs and SAMs that still presented a lethal threat.

Having quickly refuelled from a nearby tanker, Thorsness had no choice but to head back into the fray – he had promised himself that he would never lose a wingman. Over the rescue site he broke through cloud and found himself entering a 'wagon wheel' (Lufbery circle) formation of five MiG-17s. Thorsness fired off his last burst of 20 mm ammunition;

'I was able to track the MiG using 30 degrees of bank. I placed the pipper ahead and above the MiG and opened fire at an estimated 2000 ft. I allowed my pipper to slowly slide through the upper wing of the MiG. After 2.5 seconds of firing the MiG evidently saw our aircraft, for he tightened his turn to the left. I observed some large pieces coming off the aircraft. Shortly afterwards I also observed two fuel tanks spraying fuel as they descended.'

Thorsness' gun-camera film had run out so this was officially counted as a 'probable' kill, although Maj Frederick G Tolman in 'Nitro' strike flight witnessed the engagement and also saw smoke streaming from the MiG.

Once again 'Kingfish 1' then had to outrun MiGs and then return to the scene. Permission to bring in rescue helicopters was repeatedly delayed because of uncertainty about the MiGs, the status of 'Kingfish 2's' crew and persistent communications problems. As the 'Sandy' aircraft approached and the MiGs responded, Thorsness made a series of runs at the VPAF fighters at tree-top level, but sadly Maj John Hamilton's slow-moving A-1E ('Sandy 01') had already been hit by MiG gunfire and he was killed when the aircraft crashed into a rocky outcrop. Thorsness and Johnson continued their one-aeroplane war until another F-105 flight came to relieve them and allow them a second in-flight refuelling opportunity. They then heard that the rescue had been abandoned and the second 'Sandy' had gone home. Ironically, just minutes earlier, the rescue control centre ('Brigham') had finally allowed 'Panda' flight of F-105Ds to cover the rescue site and protect the helicopters, but it was too late.

Meanwhile, the rest of the strike force had been fully occupied over the Xuan Mai target area. 'Nitro' flight followed the 'Kingfish' *Iron Hand* flight in over the barracks, delivering its M117 bombs and encountering 11 MiGs. Maj Jack W Hunt ('Nitro 1') saw four of them

– three were camouflaged – approaching his aircraft in two pairs, and he gave the order to jettison ordnance, although only 'Nitro 2' and '4' did so. 'Nitro 3' (Maj Tolman) did not see the VPAF fighters, and thought the MiG call referred to the single jet that they had just seen firing at 'Kingfish 2'. He therefore decided to keep his bombs, partly because the flight's speed was 200 knots above the safe jettison speed.

Hunt's element broke away to the right towards the MiGs, narrowly avoiding a collision with Tolman's element, which continued straight ahead to the target with 'Nitro 4'. Maj Hunt then bombed the target, with his bomb-less wingman beside him. Turning back to cover the other 'Nitro' pair as they bombed, they saw two MiGs ahead of them. Hunt lit his 'blower' and cut one of the MiGs off in its turn, firing an AIM-9B with a good launch tone when he was within range. The missile could not match the MiG's rate of turn, however, and it passed 200 ft behind the fighter as the jet escaped interception. Maj Tolman noticed another MiG-17 on 'Nitro 1's' tail and he cleaned off his tanks and bomb rack for a stern attack. Suddenly, the MiG pilot performed a favourite, disconcerting turn manoeuvre that instantly reversed the situation and placed him on Tolman's tail within seconds. Once again the J75 afterburner saved Tolman's element, which left the MiG far behind.

With fuel and ammunition still aboard, 'Nitro' flight reformed and decided to return in search of more of the MiGs, whose pilots might well have thought the fight was over. Hunt saw a camouflaged MiG-17, and he accelerated to within 600 ft of it, firing 200 rounds from behind the fighter. Although there was no visible impact, he felt sure the MiG was damaged. Moments later Tolman's sharp eyes again detected a MiG on his leader's tail, which he in turn pursued. It made a hard descending turn, which Tolman tried to follow, but the MiG was soon turning towards him for a head-on attack. He fired a long burst from 1500 ft down to 100 ft, and saw shells exploding all over the enemy fighter as it flew through the 'hose' of bullets;

'I fired approximately 300 rounds and observed hits around his canopy section. The MiG passed by my aircraft, going to my "six o'clock" position. I engaged afterburner and performed a high-climbing turn for re-engagement. Upon sighting the MiG again I noted a trail of white smoke coming from his tailpipe. I saw him roll slowly to the left and start a gentle descent.'

Pieces were seen to fly off the MiG, and Tolman's gun camera later confirmed the kill.

There were still plenty more VPAF fighters in the area, and Tolman saw another one heading northwest at about 1500 ft. He took his element down to treetop height and advanced in intermittent afterburner to a favourable position behind and below the MiG for an AIM-9B shot at it against a sky background – the ideal conditions for the missile. His attempt was

Maj Hunt's F-105D 58-1168 with the 354th TFS in reverse camouflage, photographed prior to downing a MiG. Cartridge-starting the J75 engine was standard at Thai bases due to the pace of activities and the number of aircraft per mission. A large pyrotechnic device combusted instantly, creating hot gases that started the turbine spinning, ready for ignition of the fuel. Dense, choking fumes often entered the open cockpit, and a misfire could cause internal fire damage (*USAF*)

F-105D 62-4384 ended its career with the Virginia ANG, this jet having been used by Maj Fred Tolman on 19 April 1967 to destroy a MiG-17. As 354th TFS chief tactics consultant and subsequently squadron weapons officer, 'Ted' Tolman had developed, with Maj Ken Bell, the 355th TFW's practice of 'offensive withdrawal'. This meant attacking extra ground targets of opportunity or MiGs on the exit routes after bombing their primary targets (*via Peter Schinkelshoek*)

frustrated by yet another MiG-17 that approached them from the left. 'Nitro 4' called a break but Tolman apparently did not hear the warning due to excessive radio traffic, so his wingman broke away, pursued by the MiG. The pilot of the aircraft targeted by Maj Tolman probably received radio warning of his presence, since he broke away sharply just as the AIM-9B was about to be launched. Tolman attempted to follow him, and resorted to his 20 mm gun, which fired sporadically and appeared to score one hit on the MiG's right wing. After Tolman had overshot the target the gun started to behave again, so he returned to the fray once more, hoping for another chance.

Maj Hunt and his wingman, meanwhile, were nearby, flying at 500 knots and 5000 ft, when they detected a MiG-17 heading north below them. Hunt dived onto the MiG's tail for his third engagement of the day and saw it start to jink as he closed to within 3000 ft and began to fire short bursts. From 1500 ft Hunt saw 'numerous hits and flashes coming from the top of the fuselage just behind the canopy. My pipper [gunsight] at this firing position was just forward and a little high on his canopy. I observed no large pieces of material coming from his aircraft.'

The F-105D's gun camera did not work and Hunt was unable to see the MiG after it dived away to the right, trailing smoke, so he assumed it was a 'probable' kill. However, other sources confirmed the loss later in the day.

Although 'Nitro 1' and '2' had to head for home after claiming this kill, Fred Tolman was still MiG hunting. He spotted a silver MiG-17 slowly circling a field near Hoa Binh on which its pilot may have been contemplating a landing. As Tolman approached, the VPAF pilot pulled up into a climbing manoeuvre that his opponent could not follow closely enough to secure a good Sidewinder tone. The 'Thud' pilot nevertheless yanked the nose of his fighter up in a 7g turn and fired his last few rounds, with the MiG partly obscured under his aircraft's nose.

Tolman felt himself 'greying out' with the crushing g-forces, but he saw the MiG begin to emerge into his line of vision. He fired his AIM-9B at a range of about 200 ft, hoping for a lucky hit, but did not see the result as he overshot the MiG and passed through its jet-wash at close range. The turbulence tore his hand off the control column and forced his head down violently, causing him to lose control until he could pull out of a dive below 500 ft. Tolman reckoned that he was the last F-105 in the area by that stage, and he also heard the F-4C MiGCAP pilots calling a 'bogie'

– possibly himself. With less than 1000 lbs of fuel left he refuelled and returned to Takhli with a deep four-inch gouge in his aircraft's windscreen, probably caused by debris from the first MiG fight.

The last Thunderchiefs in action over Xuan Mai were from 'Panda' flight. Carrying M117 bombs, it was the second strike flight to hit the Xuan Mai barracks. Two MiG-17s were spotted as the F-105s left the target, the 'Thud' pilots cleaning off their tanks and MERs and accelerating to 600 knots behind the unsuspecting VPAF pilots. As 'Panda 1' (Capt William 'Gene' Eskew) prepared to fire from 1500 ft the MiG element turned sharply towards the target area. Eskew adjusted his position, but as he reached for the trigger again he was distracted by another flight of Takhli F-105s that suddenly approached head on, just above 'Panda'. However, he re-acquired the MiGs over Hoa Binh and was able to fire at one from a distance of about 800 ft. With his gunsight and radar properly set up, Eskew saw bullets explode on the jet's left wing root. His wingman, Capt Paul Seymour, also scored hits on a second MiG, but both enemy fighters turned sharply and escaped. Eskew reported, 'It was absolutely impossible for us to follow them through that turn'.

Another MiG-17 was seen moments later, and its pilot rapidly acquired a position behind them within perfect gun range. Afterburners were lit and 450-gallon tanks jettisoned into the MiG's flightpath, causing the VPAF jet to lose some speed and fall behind. 'Panda' flight duly withdrew and refuelled from a 'Green Anchor' tanker, although 'Panda 4' required assistance to do so. Fortunately, Leo Thorsness was on hand to provide this. Whilst arranging for a tanker hook-up over Laos for his own fuel-starved aircraft, he heard a distress call from 'Panda 4' stating that he was lost, with only 600 lbs of fuel. Putting aside his own urgent fuel requirement, Thorsness guided the tanker and 'Panda 4' into a link-up just as the F-105D's engine was about to flame out over enemy territory.

He then took his own aircraft up to 35,000 ft, calculated that a Thunderchief could glide two miles for every 1000 ft of altitude and set the throttle to idle for the last 70 miles of the journey. The engine cut out as the F-105F touched down at Udorn RTAFB after what Capt Johnson modestly described as a 'full day's work', marred by the capture of the 'Kingfish 2' crew. Maj Thorsness was awarded the Medal of Honor, but by the time this was announced he was already a prisoner of war in Hanoi.

As they approached their KC-135A, the other members of 'Panda' flight heard that 'Kingfish 2' was down, but they did not hear any mention of air cover for the RESCAP effort. Eskew offered the services of 'Panda' flight, only to be told that their short endurance (as they had jettisoned their external tanks) would reduce their effectiveness – external tanks were normally carried by RESCAP aircraft. It soon became obvious that they were the only aircraft available though, and the *Red*

In-flight refuelling with flying boom-equipped tankers took around six minutes to fill the F-105's tanks at 4500 lbs per minute. The first aircraft in the flight had to return for a top-up before the flight departed, as it would have used the equivalent of one underwing tank full of fuel while waiting for the other three to refuel. External tanks were usually jettisoned if engagement with MiGs was imminent as they limited the aircraft's manoeuvrability. 34th TFS F-105D 62-4347 (closest to the camera), flown by MiG-killer Maj Donald Russell, ended its career as the 'High Time Thud' with a record 6730.5 flying hours by 1983 (*via Peter Schinkelshoek*)

Crown controller allowed them to refuel and make the 200-mile return journey to the target area. As they re-entered the arena Maj Thorsness had warned them of the MiGs, and advised them that he had to leave as his fuel was very low.

The surviving RESCAP 'Sandy' A-1E was still under attack by four MiG-17s when 'Panda' flight arrived. The MiGs, three of them flown by VPAF officers Tan, Tho and Trung, attacked in a 'butterfly' pattern of carefully coordinated individual passes. 'Sandy 02' jettisoned his stores but hung onto an SUU-11/A 7.62 mm gun pod, which he fired head-on at a MiG from 500 ft, booting his rudder to make the bullets disperse. Other than that he had only the slow-speed manoeuvrability of his heavy, piston-engined aircraft at treetop altitude to steer clear of the five firing passes the MiGs had made by the time the 'Panda' Thunderchiefs roared in to the rescue at 700 knots.

'Sandy 02' saw their approach and talked them in towards him, but he also noticed another MiG-17 close behind them and called for them to, 'Break! One of those fuckers is on your tail!' Rather than selecting one of the circling MiGs as a target, Gene Eskew elected to drive 'Panda' flight straight through them at supersonic speed in an effort to disperse them. One of the MiG pilots quickly recovered and turned in behind Seymour's F-105D. Capt Howard Bodenhamer ('Panda 3') in turn rolled in behind the MiG. Another VPAF jet moved in behind him, and that was soon followed by 'Panda 4' (Capt Robert Hammerle) in a frantic line astern chase. Eskew had noticed yet another MiG heading away north towards Hoa Lac airfield, presumably fuel-starved, and he pulled in behind it and fired his AIM-9B. The missile's proximity fuse may not have had time to arm since it passed five feet beneath the MiG's wing without detonating in conditions that were otherwise ideal for a Sidewinder.

Turning back to the 'furball', Eskew saw Bodenhamer's gunfire hitting the lead MiG and heard Hammerle warning Bodenhamer (who had slowed to 275 knots in a 6g turn to track his target) that he was under fire from another MiG. Bodenhamer hung on and fired, hitting the MiG-17 on its left wing and just behind the canopy (witnessed by Eskew). He then had to react to the large, orange fireballs passing close to his canopy, wrestling the sluggish F-105 into a break. With full rudder and a steep dive, he persuaded it to descend into a cloud, hoping there was no karst rock inside it.

Hammerle, meanwhile, continued to fire at 'Panda 3's' pursuing MiG from only 200 ft behind it, but no hits were evident. Eskew, watching the shells pumping from 'Panda 4's' gun, could not understand why the MiG was not burning. 'Panda 4' was now in trouble himself, Hammerle transmitting, 'Somebody help me. I have a MiG on my tail and I can't shake him'. Eskew, with no one on his tail, was able to switch his armament from 'Missiles-Air' to 'Guns-Air' and pull in behind Hammerle's adversary. He drove it off with a quick burst of 20 mm fire, executing a high-speed yo-yo manoeuvre to avoid overshooting, and then resumed firing at the MiG.

Eskew reported, 'I saw an estimated 50 to 75 hits on the upper fuselage directly behind the canopy'. The MiG-17 began a slow roll, forcing the F-105 pilot to pull up hard to avoid a collision. Seconds later his aircraft was engulfed by fire as the MiG disintegrated in a violent explosion. Eskew's head jerked down onto his chest, as he feared that his jet was going to be hit by debris. Convinced he had rammed the MiG, he transmitted,

'I hit him. "Panda lead" is hit'. However, when he had had a moment to check his aircraft he found that the tough Thunderchief was actually undamaged, so he went back into the fight. 'Glancing back at the downed MiG, I saw the wreckage burning on the ground. I could see the smoke from both "Sandy 01" and the MiG'. The surviving VPAF fighters were still attempting to destroy 'Sandy 02', who was desperately manoeuvring around the karst. 'Panda' flight made a more determined effort to take the MiGs' attention, allowing 'Sandy 02' to escape under low cloud.

The fight continued, with 'Pandas' and MiGs manoeuvring between 3000 ft and 30 ft. Bodenhamer saw an F-105 (probably Seymour's) hitting one of the persistent MiGs, but being pursued by two others, one of which was fired at by Eskew. Bodenhamer then fired an AIM-9B at another MiG, watching it guide directly towards the fighter's tailpipe before he had to break away to avoid another MiG. He hassled with the incoming jet in repeated scissors manoeuvres, rather than outrunning it, so as to distract attention from 'Sandy 02'. The two pilots ended up line abreast, looking at each other and wondering what to do next. They then attempted to roll across each other to get on each other's tail. In the end Bodenhamer had to play his ace. His aircraft was slowing down more than the MiG, so he engaged afterburner.

At that moment Eskew called for 'Panda' flight to disengage, and Bodenhamer accelerated to 600 knots, leaving the MiG pilot far behind as he headed into the mountains. He had 1000 lbs of fuel left, and when the flight finally reached a tanker, which had come to meet them with its throttles firewalled, he was down to 30 seconds of powered flying time remaining. The other 'Panda' aircraft were only slightly better off. Although they all returned to Takhli intact, there was general disappointment that none of their gun cameras had worked, leaving insufficient evidence for the damaged claims by 'Pandas 2', '3' and '4' to be increased to kills. Had film indeed been available, this could well have increased the F-105's MiG kill record by at least two, and raised the 19 April tally to six destroyed.

In one of the more bizarre 'near misses' of the day the leader of one of the later strike flights saw MiGs as he came off the target, and he pursued one, firing as he did so. Seconds later he realised that the MiG he thought he was chasing was actually coming towards him head-on! He abandoned the encounter.

Paul Seymour was later involved in another MiG kill by Maj Robert Rilling on 13 May that year, but the next two 355th TFW victories came on 28 April during raids on the Han Phong causeway, 12 miles from Hanoi. The preceding nine days had included several very brief glimpses of MiGs and a few inconclusive engagements. An *Iron Hand* flight leaving its target tangled with two MiG-17s close to 'Thud Ridge' on 24 April, and the lead F-105F opened fire with the gunsight still in air-to-ground mode. The cannon fired two bursts, but through only one of its six barrels, and no damage was seen.

The following day brought much greater MiG activity when a vital Hanoi electrical transformer site (JCS 82.24) was hit. 'Knife' flight from Takhli, led by Maj Ken Bell, showed that a 600-knot run to the target could frustrate the MiGs' GCI when an attempted ambush by six MiG-17s failed after their controllers turned them toward the F-105 formation too late to catch up. Instead, they moved in on the following 'Crab' flight. 1Lt Robert Weskamp ('Crab 2'), whose brother was flying one of the KC-135As for the strike, was lost over the target when his 2000-lb bombs broke loose during a high-G pitch-up and severely damaged the underside of both wings of F-105D 62-4294. He was too low for recovery or ejection. Nearby, 'Crab 3' evaded several silver MiGs when he became separated from the flight.

The mission's Korat flak suppression flight was also attacked by MiG-17s, and one F-105 pilot was interested to note that when a VPAF fighter he was following saw him and turned to get onto his tail, the MiG pilot had completed 150 degrees of his turn before he had managed 25 degrees!

During the re-attack the following day a *Wild Weasel* F-105F was destroyed by three SA-2s, but Maj Al Lenski, on his first Route Pack VI mission, got a shot at a MiG-17 after his flight leader, Capt Buddy Jones, suffered a gun jam. With a gunsight set at 40 mils (depressed) for bombing, Lenski fired at the MiG when it was about 1200 ft ahead of him. 'Ruddering' the F-105 to disperse the shots, he saw no hits before the fighter was driven away. He then had the extraordinary experience of crossing Phuc Yen airfield at 200 ft and 500 knots, meeting a MiG-21 head on and realising that it had its undercarriage extended for final approach to landing. Although they passed very close to each other, Maj Lenski had to ignore the VPAF fighter ahead of him in order to fend off a MiG-17 that was firing at him from behind.

The Han Phong mission on 28 April was opposed by MiG-17s after bombing. In addition to the usual three or four MiGs catching the F-105s as they pulled up from dive-attacks, groups of three made concerted head-on passes that the Americans found hard to counter. For the MiG pilots it was a way of improving the chances of their heavy, but scattered, shells hitting something. The leading F-105 flight actually outmanoeuvred the first group of MiGs and returned fire against the second trio, without registering any hits.

'Spitfire' flight, which was the first into the target with M118s, was harassed by numerous MiG-17s. Inbound, it avoided the first MiG flight, but a major dogfight with at least nine more developed as they left the target. The flight leader, Maj Harry E 'Hank' Higgins, noticed a MiG ahead of him and manoeuvred until he was behind it. During these contortions he managed to set up an AIM-9B and fire it from 3000 ft. However, while he was concentrating on the pre-launch switchology in the cockpit the MiG turned and flew away from him. The VPAF pilot had obviously seen the Sidewinder's distinctive corkscrew trail and turned tightly so that the missile passed 1000 ft behind him. Higgins and his wingman for 50 previous missions, 1Lt Gordon Jenkins, then continued out towards Laos, at which point they were involved in a head-on shoot-out with two more MiGs, again without achieving any visible results.

F-105D 59-1772, with starter cartridge fumes billowing from an underfuselage vent, has MiG kill markings for both Col Bob Scott and Maj Harry 'Hank' Higgins. Col Scott flew in World War 2, Korea and Vietnam, totalling more than 300 missions (134 of them over North Vietnam). His personal call-sign was 'Scotch 1 Bags a MiG'. Higgins also had considerable fighter experience (*via Col Jack Broughton*)

Col Arthur Dennis flew F-105D 60-0504 on 28 April 1967 for his aerial victory. Delivered to the 36th TFW in October 1961, it arrived at Takhli RTAFB in March 1967 after further service with the 4th, 18th and 23rd TFWs. Capt Thomas Lesan claimed another (unconfirmed) MiG kill in it later in 1967. The jet was subsequently nicknamed *Memphis Belle II*, these markings being reinstated when it was placed on display within the National Museum of the USAF at Wright-Patterson AFB, Ohio, in 1990 (*via Paul Osborne collection*)

Returning to their planned egress route, Higgins then spotted another MiG heading south and engaged afterburner to follow it. He reported;

'I completed the switch settings for guns and began to close. The MiG tightened his turn, but was slow in doing so. This allowed me to gain a 30-degree cut-off angle, and when I was approximately 1500 ft behind the jet I began to fire. As I prolonged the firing I noticed that the MiG had begun to smoke, and flames erupted from his left wing-root [an image that was recorded on his aircraft's nose-mounted KA-71 strike camera]. He began a steep descending turn with the left wing down at approximately 1000 ft. My last glance at him showed him burning and spiralling down at less than 500 ft.'

Higgins and Jenkins were then chased by two more MiGs, their noses flashing with cannon fire as the F-105 pilots accelerated away from them in a dive. At this point Higgins and Jenkins decided to shed their centreline fuel tanks, as more MiGs had been sighted. They had to evade three more attacks before they could exit the area. Despite both pilots being fired at by ten MiGs, they returned home undamaged. Once again gun camera film was available as part of the evidence to confirm Higgins' aerial success.

'Atlanta' flight from the 355th TFW was providing flak suppression for the mission, with four F-105Ds carrying CBU dispensers. It arrived six minutes after the first flight in line abreast 'pod' formation and delivered the ordnance. Turning to leave, the flight leader, Lt Col Arthur F Dennis, saw a MiG-17 ahead of them threatening an F-105F from the *Iron Hand* flight that had arrived at the same time as 'Atlanta' and launched four Shrikes at SAM sites. The *Wild Weasels* had been involved in a sustained gunfight with three MiG-17s, and the flight leader had hit one in the wing. Lt Col Dennis ordered afterburner for the flight to catch up with the MiG and set up an AIM-9B. Although it had a good tone, the missile failed to guide and wandered off to the left.

Having ascertained that the Sidewinder would not home onto the F-105F, Dennis re-set the switches for 20 mm cannon while his wingman closed in on the MiG's tail and fired 277 rounds from an ideal position. There were no hits, possibly because his gunsight was set up for 'missiles-air'. In a 3g turn he attempted a second burst, only for his gun to jam. Lt Col Dennis resumed his firing position and opened up at a distance of more than 3000 ft and 550 knots;

'The MiG was by this time in a shallow right turn, level, and apparently did not see me because he did not attempt evasive action. I continued closing to approximately 1500 ft, when I began firing, and closed to 700 ft and the MiG burst into a large ball of flames. It continued to burn and trail smoke as it went into a steeper turn and nosed over into a wide spiral towards the ground.'

'Atlanta' flight then had to exit after SAM warnings.

The VPAF pilots' retaliation came hours later when two MiG-17s and two MiG-21s intercepted a flak suppression flight that had separated into two elements. The lead section met two MiG-17s as it exited along 'Thud Ridge' and turned towards them, but the communist fighters vanished into the haze and low cloud. The second element was flying about 60 miles ahead (slowed down somewhat by a CBU that had hung up on the No 4 aircraft), and the leader transmitted, 'They are coming at us'. The MiG-21s hit both aircraft with cannon fire in two passes, which the Thunderchief pilots were unable to avoid. F-105D 58-1151, flown by Capt Franklin Caras, crashed in flames and he ejected but did not survive. His wingman's aircraft was damaged in its airbrake section. Caras's jet was the only F-105 lost to the guns of a MiG-21.

The last day of April proved to be even worse for the 355th TFW. In yet another attack on JCS 82.24 three F-105s were lost within an hour and four crewmen taken prisoner, including Maj Thorsness and Capt Harold Johnson who were 'Carbine 3' in a flight of three F-105Fs and an F-105D. One MiG-17 was shot down.

Flying their second mission of the day, and seven missions away from completing their 'magic 100' and ending their tour, Maj Thorsness and Capt Johnson took off fearing that trouble loomed ahead. As they approached the moment to launch their Shrike missiles while travelling at a speed of 600 knots, they received a powerful air-to-air radar warning signal. Thorsness advised the F-4 Phantom II escort flight, who in turn told them that the F-105s were appearing on their radar. In fact, the warning related to two MiG-21s lurking in the valley below them, not the F-105s. MiG sightings were transmitted by both Maj Al Lenski and later by Capt Joe Ritter ('Carbine 2'), who saw Bob Abbott's aircraft hit, but they were lost in the general confusion of radio traffic and SAM warning noise.

The MiGs climbed and Le Trong Huyen fired an 'Atoll' that exploded in the tailpipe of Thorsness's F-105F with a force 'like we'd been smacked by a giant sledgehammer'. The cockpit filled with smoke, the controls ceased to operate and the crew ejected at 690 mph to begin six years of agonising captivity in Hanoi after a long but tragically unsuccessful rescue effort. 1Lt Bob Abbott, flying with them as 'Carbine 4', was also hit by an 'Atoll' from the second MiG, flown by Nguyen Ngoc Do. Abbott was captured, as was Capt Joe Abbott, a wing safety officer and No 4 in 'Tomahawk' flight, which was flying a RESCAP orbit for the other downed crews. His F-105D was the first in a series of nine claimed kills credited to Nguyen Van Coc that made him the foremost MiG-21 ace. These 30 April successes for the VPAF also proved that the F-105 was very vulnerable to a well-flown MiG-21 under skilful GCI. Al Lenski's aircraft was also damaged by an 'Atoll'.

The morning mission on 30 April, which Thorsness and Johnson had also flown, was part of the onslaught on North Vietnam's rail transportation. The mission's third strike flight was 'Rattler', led by Capt Tom Lesan. The 'Rattler' F-105s came under fire from three MiG-17s as they prepared to deliver their M117s. However, the pilots raced on to the target at a speed that the MiGs could not match. Having released his six bombs, Lesan cleaned off his 450-gallon tanks and adjusted his sights for air-to-air guns as he went after the MiGs with a 100-knot overtake speed. 'As I started to track the No 2 MiG', he reported, 'they both started a rolling, descending turn to the right, and I followed, rolling to about 12 degrees. I tracked and opened fire at approximately 1000 ft. I fired 100 rounds, noting hits impacting down the left side of the forward fuselage and on the left wing. With such a great rate of closure I had to break left to avoid collision. I rolled right and observed the MiG slowly levelling out with his left wing in flames'.

Lesan had to estimate his lead angle on the MiG using the pitot boom on the F-105's nose because he was pulling 4g as he fired and the pipper on his gunsight had moved right off the combining glass, indicating that he should not fire. However, his wingman, Maj James H Middleton Jnr, soon saw the burning MiG spinning towards the ground.

Col Broughton organised a further rescue effort for Joe Abbott, as well as a MiG sweep, very early on 1 May. It was one of the few occasions when F-105s were configured exclusively for air-to-air MiG hunting, each jet carrying wing tanks, two AIM-9Bs and a full load of 20 mm ammunition. 'We decided to leave the bombs at home since we weren't after ground targets on this one', Broughton recalled.

Although the weather was too bad to advance the recovery of Abbott, the leading flight found eight MiG-17s and a determined dogfight ensued. The VPAF pilots flew defensively, concentrating on keeping F-105s off their tails and constantly using tight turns to deny their counterparts from the 355th TFW anything more than quick snapshot bursts and an AIM-9B launch in unfavourable parameters. The Thunderchief pilots avoided being drawn into low-speed turning manoeuvres, and no visible damage occurred, although morale at Takhli was somewhat restored by this determined attempt to punish the MiG units.

F-4C Phantom IIs, which had been 'bombed up' to join strike flights because of low MiG activity, were returned to CAP duties. It was found that inserting an F-4 flight between the F-105 flights, with another at the rear of the formation, provided the best protection against MiGs. In other operations from then until 12 May VPAF fighters attacked several F-105 flights with quick hit-and-run tactics using guns or unguided rockets, but they did not stay to fight. However, May 1967 proved to be a disastrous month for the VPAF.

Capt Thomas Lesan's MiG killer (60-0498) lived on to operate with the Virginia ANG's 149th TFS as *Top Dog*. Lesan's successful MiG-17 attack involved a combination of the gunsight and eyeball-based estimation. Close-in firing from behind the target was one of the F-105's advantages compared with the Phantom II until the latter received gun pods or, in the F-4E, an internally mounted cannon (*via Peter Schinkelshoek*)

MAY MASSACRE

USAF fighter crews destroyed 26 VPAF MiGs in 35 aerial engagements during May 1967 for the loss of just two F-4C Phantom IIs to MiG-17s. Six of the communist jets fell to F-105 pilots. Although MiG activity had steadily increased, effective defensive activity by the USAF strike packages considerably reduced the ordnance-jettisoning incidents. Long-standing restrictions on attacking MiG air bases had been lifted on 23 April and several fighters were destroyed on the ground at Kep and Hoa Lac.

'Crossbow' was a 333rd TFS flak suppression flight on 12 May for an attack near Phuc Yen airfield, its F-105s being armed with M117s and AIM-9Bs. Flight leader Capt Jacques A Suzanne saw four MiG-17s attacking 'Warhawk' strike flight ahead of him and he accelerated after the enemy fighters, tracking two MiGs that turned to the right. From 4000 ft and an angle-off approaching 60 degrees, he fired 200 rounds in air-to-ground mode. Reversing his turn, the MiG pilots dived away to the left and Capt Suzanne fired another 200 rounds, this time with 90 degrees angle-off and minimum range. White smoke streamed from a MiG as it dived away into broken cloud. 'Crossbow 2' (Capt Lawrence D Cobb), who also fired a short burst at it, saw an explosion on the ground when the MiG crashed.

Saturday, May 13 was as unlucky a day for the VPAF as 2 January (Operation *Bolo*) had been. Seven MiG-17s were shot down by two MiGCAP Phantom IIs and five F-105Ds during heavy raids on the Yen Vien railway yards and Vinh Yen barracks. An aerial battle developed between MiGs and F-105s over the target, which was joined by a 433rd TFS MiGCAP flight that was departing the area but turned back when it became aware of the dogfight. The F-4 crews quickly destroyed two MiG-17s that were pursuing F-105s.

F-105D 60-0497 *MISS T* was Maj 'Mo' Seaver's mount on 13 May 1967 when he shot down a MiG-17. Seaver had a long-established reputation as a hell raiser and practical joker. He ejected from F-105s twice and returned to the war in command of an F-111A wing. The F-105 APR-25/26 ECM system, visible under the nose and on the upper tailfin, was installed within a six-week period in March-April 1966. The fighter is seen here with a seldom carried, drag-inducing twin Sidewinder launcher. The warhead of the AIM-9B exploded into 1500 high-density fragments, travelling at 6000 ft per second, that could penetrate one-inch aluminium sheet up to 30 ft away. The weapon's overall hit rate up to 1967 was 18.6 per cent, although only 26 per cent of the missiles were launched outside design parameters (*Larsen/Taylor*)

CHAPTER FIVE

Maj Maurice 'Mo' Seaver was 'Tamale 1' in the last of four flights to bomb Vinh Yen. Leaving the target, he noticed a camouflaged aircraft below him. Most MiGs were silver, so he waited for a visual ID, which came when he saw the red stars on its wings. It was the first MiG he had seen, despite having flown 4000 hours in Tactical Air Command aircraft. Closing in behind the MiG, Seaver decided that its pilot was concentrating on other F-105s and had not seen him. He opened fire, saw no hits and quickly realised the usual problem – his gunsight was still set to 126 mils for bombing. As Seaver began to readjust it the MiG reversed its turn and the F-105 pilot had to turn hard to stay with it. With no time to set up an AIM-9, he fired his cannon ahead of the MiG by calculated guesswork. He saw the fighter pass through his 20 mm bullets that cut into its wing and nose. It made a sharp right turn, there was an explosion in its right wing and its destruction was recorded by gun camera film. Seaver estimated that the whole encounter lasted less than 90 seconds.

The 355th TFW's intense battles over Yen Vien involved the first successes for AIM-9Bs fired from Thunderchiefs. 'Chevrolet' flight led 20 F-105s along the 15 miles of protection offered by 'Thud Ridge' (which rose to 5000 ft in places) and past Phuc Yen to the target in pod formation, almost line abreast. They were uninterrupted en route to the target, but three MiG-17s were seen ten miles ahead. As Lt Col Gast ('Chevrolet' lead) turned his flight behind them, the MiGs swung round for a head-on attack. As the two flights hurtled towards each other both Gast and Capt Charlie Couch ('Chevrolet 3') set up their single AIM-9Bs. Gast did not have a tone on his missile and he fired it from 7000 ft in an effort to break up the MiG formation. It expired 200 ft from the enemy fighters. Couch realised the detection tone 'growl' from his Sidewinder was probably due to the sun directly ahead, so he held fire.

As the distance closed to 3000 ft both pilots opened up with 20 mm cannon fire. The two flights met and crossed 300 ft apart, and 'Chevrolet 2' (Maj Alonzo L Ferguson) later reported, 'As I looked to the rear [after the MiGs passed below] I noted a grey cloud of smoke, tinged with pink, receding in the distance'. Lt Col Gast trusted that the dispersion of his bullets in a circle of 15-20 ft from a distance of 3000 ft would have compensated for his incorrectly adjusted gunsight. Pilots in the following F-105 flight saw a pilot eject from the smoking MiG and another MiG-17 falling away in a spin. In Capt Couch's view, 'The MiG I was firing at took violent evasive action to avoid a head-on collision and very likely could have entered a spin'. Both Gast and Couch were awarded kills during these, their third MiG engagements, and 97th and 82nd missions respectively.

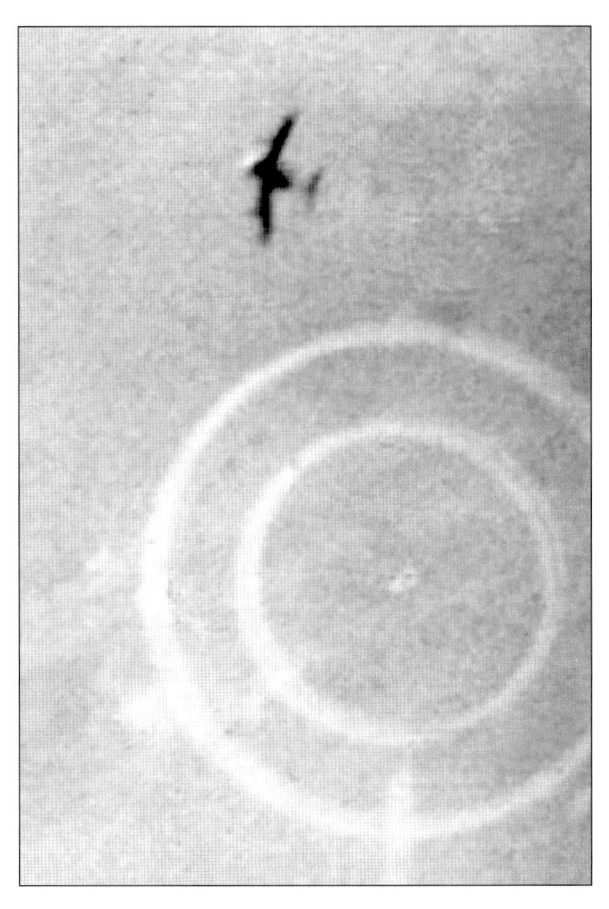

A frame from Maj Seaver's gun camera film during his successful MiG-17 engagement of 13 May 1967 (*USAF*)

Maj Seaver (centre), with Maj Robert Piper (with 'bulletproof' moustache) and Capts Jim Chambers and Bill Kriz (right) after their 100th mission 'dunking' in the 388th TFW swimming pool at Korat. Bill Kriz recalled, '"Mo" Seaver, "Bear" Chambers, Bob Piper and I were all on our 100th mission together in Route Pack V. It should have been relatively safe, but it was the closest I came to being hit. On the way down the chute a red fireball passed within ten feet of my windscreen at "12 o'clock". Back at Korat, we made a line abreast pass down the runway prior to landing. All available squadron vehicles came out to meet us at the end of the runway and escort us to the revetments, red flares and flags a-flying. The 44th TFS had a baby blue howitzer, which all four of us mounted and we were towed to the base swimming pool. Then came the required dunking. The idea was to see how many of the "dunkers" one could pull in also. At 5 ft 6 in and weighing just 140 lbs, I didn't pose much of a problem' (*USAF*)

'Random' flight, led by Maj Robert G Rilling, was a few minutes behind 'Chevrolet' in the same attack, and it too ran into two Lufbery circles of MiG-17s at both high and low altitudes as it left the target and egressed along 'Thud Ridge'. Rilling called for an attack and Maj Carl D Osborne ('Random 3') lit his afterburner and set up his Sidewinder as the flight accelerated into the MiGs' rear quarter. He rolled in behind the second enemy fighter and heard a good AIM-9B tone. Rilling also powered up a Sidewinder, aiming for the lead MiG-17. His missile flew accurately, detonating very close to the jet's tail. Large chunks of structure fell away in a trail of grey smoke. 'I followed the jet through a 180-degree left turn in an attempt to use the Vulcan cannon', Rilling explained. 'After completing that manoeuvre the MiG rolled hard right and down and impacted the ground'.

Osborne's target started a left turn, but with only 1g on his aircraft he was able to track the target and fire his AIM-9B from 4000 ft;

'I rolled into a slight right bank and the tone on the AIM-9 peaked up normally. Only a ten-degree left bank was required to hold the [gunsight] reticle on the MiG. I fired the missile and it began tracking and detonated at the MiG's "three-four o'clock" position. He immediately turned left and began trailing smoke. My lead [Maj Rilling] called that he had also scored a hit on the other MiG. I made a hard left turn and observed the MiG I had fired at still trailing smoke and descending.

'My turn caused a great loss of airspeed and allowed a third MiG-17 to turn inside me by the time I had completed 180 degrees. The MiG was now at my "nine o'clock" position, and it began firing. I didn't believe he was either in range of me, or had any lead on me. However, my wingman was in a more vulnerable position, so I dropped the nose and unloaded the Gs and began accelerating to 550-600 knots. As I began to dive I saw the MiG stop firing and the pilot break to his right and away from my element. He would have been in a good position to make a pass on myself and "Random 4", but I saw Capt Seymour, who had lagged in the left climbing turn and stayed low, in a good firing position on this MiG. He was firing, but I was unable to assess any damage by Seymour except that my attacker broke off and stopped firing.'

An F-105 in a later flight saw the tail of Osborne's target MiG fall off and he then witnessed the jet crashing. Seymour, who had joined Rilling's flight after becoming separated from his own, claimed hits on the MiG's fuselage and wing, and also witnessed the successes of Osborne and Rilling.

On 13 May the MiGs had attempted to set up one aircraft as 'bait' for the American fighters, with three other jets positioned to attack from behind. Good formation keeping and alert wingmen generally foiled these tactics, although faster, less visible MiG-21s could still deploy these traps successfully. Despite effective 'pod' formations, SAMs still posed a real threat when aircraft split up for bombing runs. SAMs, and the rigid formation tactics adopted to defeat them, also cost F-105 pilots potential MiG kills. For example, the leader of a Ha Dong strike flight on 14 May would have been able to attack two silver MiG-17s as he came off target but for a concerted SAM attack that forced the entire flight to jettison its bombs. To make matters worse, the leader's wingman, Maj G R Wilson, was shot down by a SAM. As the missile barrage continued any attempt at engaging the VPAF fighters was abandoned. Five MiGs also attacked the *Iron Hand* flight that same day and three were shot down by Phantom IIs.

In a more formal setting, Maj Seaver, still wearing his parachute, is congratulated by Brig Gen Edwin F Black upon his return from his 100th mission. Above Seaver's head is the unique F-105 air intake. Derived from NACA-tested work on the XF-103 interceptor, this variable air inlet had an automatically adjusted 'plug' inside it to modify its cross-sectional area and regulate the airflow throughout the speed range. It was highly efficient and it improved the aircraft's acceleration (*USAF/HQ Seventh Air Force*)

Maj Robert Rilling flew F-105D 60-0522 (bearing two MiG kill stars here) on 13 May 1967, when he achieved the first Thunderchief MiG kill with an AIM-9B missile. Maj Carl Osborne, in the same flight, also destroyed a MiG-17 with a missile – the only time that MiGs were destroyed by F-105s using AIM-9Bs alone. When MiG-21s with Sidewinder-copy missiles approached them, the F-105 pilots' main defence was to 'hit the deck' so that heat emissions from the ground would baffle the weapons' seeker heads (*USAF*)

Maj Ralph Kuster's reverse-camouflaged *Mickey Titty Chi* (60-0424) receives attention at Korat. Kuster's 3 June 1967 MiG kill was achieved with 20 mm gunfire, while Capt Larry Wiggins used both the gun and an AIM-9B for his victory on the same day. One flight of F-105s was often tasked with defending the strike force, particularly over targets where MiGs could be expected. For example, on the 15 November 1967 strike on Phuc Yen airfield Maj Sam Armstrong, in the 34th TFS's 'Fresno' flight, saw MiGs approaching behind them and jettisoned his bombs and tanks. 'We went into afterburner and broke into the MiGs. They fired something but I never saw them again. On the way out we saw one lone MiG – silver, the other two were camouflaged – high and going away. No chance to get him. Sure was nice chasing MiGs rather than braving the flak' (*USAF*)

The Ubon MiGCAP did particularly well on 20 May, destroying four MiG-17s while 366th TFW F-4 crews downed two MiG-21s. Such effective fighter escorting allowed five F-105 flights to hit their railway yard targets as the CAP crews dealt with the 14 MiGs that threatened the strike force. With so many VPAF fighters in the air it was inevitable that there would also be skirmishes and gunfire exchanged between several F-105s and the MiGs.

Sporadic encounters continued through May that saw MiGs firing at F-105s and then breaking away and escaping when challenged, and Thunderchief pilots chasing MiGs until they turned to attack them, forcing the F-105s to accelerate away. A Korat Thunderchief pilot had a good chance of a MiG-21 kill on 22 May. He fired an AIM-9B that went ballistic and followed up with gunfire, but his Vulcan cannon malfunctioned and emitted flames that caused engine stalls when fired. 'It was just like putting my speed brakes on', he noted.

The beginning of June yielded two further kills for Korat pilots during a 16-aircraft attack on the Bac Giang Bridge – a vital link between China and Hanoi. 'Hambone' flight was the first in, delivering massive M118s through very heavy 85 mm and 100 mm AAA barrages. Maj Ralph L Kuster Jnr ('Hambone 2') fired a brief burst at the flak emplacements, hoping that his gun camera, set to overrun by three seconds, would record clues as to their locations. His flight left the target at a little over Mach 1 and advanced six miles before three MiG-17s were sighted, spaced out in trail formation, ahead of them. 'Hambone Lead' (Maj John Rowan) commenced a 180-degree left turn followed by the second and third F-105s. Moments earlier 'Hambone 4' had narrowly avoided a collision with the second F-105 flight as it egressed the target. He then lost his own flight when it turned sharply, so he decided to stay with the second flight, although his element leader, Capt Larry D Wiggins, was not aware of this.

The MiGs entered a 'wagon wheel' defensive orbit at an altitude of 500 ft, with each fighter equally spaced so that any hostile aircraft breaking into the circle could be attacked by the next MiG in line. 'Hambone' flight entered the circle, looking for a firing opportunity. 'Hambone Lead' and Wiggins ('Hambone 3') overshot in the attempt, while Kuster protected them from behind. All three pilots were by now peering through their front windscreens to try and follow the action as their canopies were fogged with condensation. Kuster eventually solved this problem by turning off his cockpit ventilation. Wiggins was still carrying his 650-gallon centreline tank as he had decided it was too risky to drop it without negative g-force on the aircraft. The other pilots released theirs at 550 knots, having found a moment to put zero g-force on their aircraft.

The MiGs loosened their turns after the first orbit at 2000 ft, flying slower than the 600 knots of the F-105s, which were varying their afterburner settings as they continued to turn. Kuster tried for another shot but the MiGs were by then in a v-formation, with the No 3 aircraft at an altitude of only 200 ft. Its pilot seemed indecisive and was rocking his wings. Wiggins, who had already set up his only AIM-9B, seized the moment by putting his gunsight pipper on the MiG's tailpipe just as its pilot ignited his afterburner – a perfect Sidewinder scenario. Although he did not have a missile tone, Wiggins fired at a range of 2500 ft in a shallow dive as his jet descended through an altitude of 1000 ft. When the missile was only 400 ft from the MiG its pilot saw the threat and began a left turn. He was banking steeply when the AIM-9B exploded beside his tailpipe. Dense white vapour began to stream out, probably from the MiG's rear fuel tank. The aircraft commenced a dive, pursued by Wiggins, who fired 376 rounds of 20 mm ammunition, with his gunsight aimed 'up and right in front of him, and I worked it right down through him'.

Although Wiggins did not see any hits, and soon overshot the MiG at high speed, the other 'Hambone' pilots saw his victim explode in a fireball and crash. Kuster recalled;

'I was watching this MiG because he was in a position to pull behind us. The MiG pulled a hard turn away from me just before the Sidewinder fused about 18 inches below his right horizontal stabiliser. Almost immediately afterwards, while he was almost perpendicular to me, he blew up in a ball of fire. I assumed "Hambone 3" had hosed him down with 20 mm rounds, which would have been one hell of a good shot.'

The remaining two MiGs were still up to a mile ahead of 'Hambone' flight, and Kuster got Maj Rowan's clearance to fire on the leading aircraft while 'Hambone 1' went for the other, which was slowing at very low altitude. Kuster fired a short burst at 45 degrees angle off while pulling

Capt Larry D Wiggins (right) uses the time-honoured pilots' 'hand language' to re-enact his 3 June 1967 MiG kill for Maj Ralph Kuster's benefit, with MiG-killing F-105D 60-0424 in the background. When the USAF began to take aerial combat seriously again in the mid-1970s, using a squadron of real MiGs, pilots were taught to manoeuvre in the vertical plane, using their excess power to beat the MiG-17's rate of turn. However, this only worked for F-4, F-104 and later fighters, since the F-105's strength lay in horizontal rather than vertical acceleration (*USAF*)

This element of F-105Ds carries a mixed complement of Mk 82 LDGP and Mk 62SE Snakeye ordnance. The lower aircraft (60-0424) was Maj Kuster's MiG killer on 3 June 1967, and also the F-105D in which 'Mo' Seaver was shot down and rescued on a 10 July 1967 *Iron Hand* mission (*USAF*)

F-105D 61-0069 was in 'Ragtop' flight on 13 May 1967, being flown by Maj Ralph Kuster, when Maj Seaver scored his MiG-17 kill. On 3 June it was Capt Wiggins' aircraft for his MiG-killing encounter, and post-war it was flown by another MiG killer, Maj Gene Basel, on a test flight at Nellis AFB. In this photograph the fighter wears the markings of the 562nd TFS/23rd TFW, which briefly returned to combat status in 1972, deploying some of its 561st TFS aircraft to Southeast Asia (*Terry Panopalis collection*)

up to 6g. His radar's air-to-air mode was not working and he was having trouble tracking the MiG through the turn, so he had to resort to a high-speed yo-yo manoeuvre to cut the overshoot rate. The MiG pilot, probably Lt Phan Tan Duan, suddenly reversed his turn, easing Kuster's difficulty and leaving the two jets running almost parallel in a left turn, with Kuster slightly behind. The MiG then turned across him again, and the F-105 pilot fired a longer burst of 20 mm ammunition in a 6g manoeuvre, running his pipper along the enemy fighter, but without hits.

As the VPAF pilot continued his turn Kuster was nearing maximum tolerable g-loads, yet he was still unable to gain enough lead on the MiG. He re-adjusted his gunsight and rapidly moved his control column fore and aft, rotating the fuselage enough to place his pipper ahead of the MiG.

One of the more graphic surviving gun camera 'stills' shows a lethal fire starting under the wing of Lt Phan Tan Duan's drop tank-equipped MiG-17 after hits by Maj Ralph Kuster, who narrowly avoided colliding with the VPAF jet as it turned into a fireball and crashed on 3 June 1967 (*USAF*)

Kuster opened fire at a range of just 200 ft, below an altitude of 700 ft, and forced the VPAF pilot to fly through the laser-stream of 20 mm rounds. An explosion under the MiG's left wing between the fuselage and the left drop tank forced Kuster to ease off his turn to avoid fire and debris that was streaming back over his aircraft. His windscreen became partly coated with melted aluminium from the MiG, and debris made an inch-wide hole inside its left air intake duct. He passed only 25 ft below the stricken VPAF fighter as it rolled inverted and smashed into the ground less than five seconds later, before an ejection was possible.

Kuster's engine began to surge violently after ingesting flames from the MiG and the Thunderchief decelerated rapidly, but the tough J75 recovered when he and Wiggins were about 30 miles from the coast en route to a tanker. 'Hambone Lead', meanwhile, had fired his AIM-9B at the MiG-17 he was following, only to see the missile suddenly lose a good tracking position and plunge earthwards.

SUMMER OF '67

The MiG pilots generally avoided F-105s for the remainder of June and July. Having taken a beating from mid-April onwards, they limited themselves to re-training and practice interceptions at a distance from US aircraft. Apart from Gia Lam (Hanoi International Airport), their six airfields were no longer safe sanctuaries (Phuc Yen was soon to be attacked also) and some of the more experienced pilots had been lost.

The use of QRC-248 equipment in 'College Eye' Lockheed EC-121D radar warning aircraft from 1967 to interrogate the IFF equipment used by the MiGs partly solved a long-standing problem. US pilots often complained about the lack of timely 'Bullseye' warnings of MiGs in their area, or of imprecision in describing the 'bandits'' location, while non-specific warnings were issued frequently, and loudly, sometimes swamping more relevant transmissions between strike flights. Mainly, this was because the EC-121s' radar could not detect or follow MiGs at low altitude. However, the ability to acquire information secretly from Soviet SRO-1 'Barly-M' IFF transponder equipment fitted in the VPAF MiGs made those warnings far more accurate.

From July 1967 the 'College Eye' aircraft were joined by a prototype EC-121K 'Rivet Top' (and EC-121Ds modified to a similar standard) fitted with QRC-248 that could monitor the conversations between MiG pilots and their ground controllers, gleaning detailed information about their activities. Unfortunately, the need to preserve secrecy when it came to using this information meant that pilots were seldom allowed to benefit from it. The VPAF, therefore, still had the decisive advantage in air combat of knowing where the enemy was and when to conduct precise surprise attacks.

On 16 August, Gen William W Momyer, Seventh Air Force commander, optimistically declared, 'We have driven the MiGs out of the sky for all practical purposes'. F-4 Phantom II MiGCAP flights were duly diverted to strike sorties, often leaving the F-105 pilots to deal with any MiGs themselves. When the latter were encountered the last Thunderchief flight was supposed to jettison its ordnance and take on 'fighter' duties. Also, some MiGCAP flights consisted only of F-105s with AIM-9Bs and gunsights pre-set to air-to-air mode for immediate aerial engagement.

Although the MiG threat had indeed been neutralised, albeit temporarily, American aircraft continued to suffer heavy losses to AAA. And in late August the VPAF units rejoined the onslaught with new tactics and in greater numbers to compensate for the reduced effectiveness of the SAM batteries due to the widespread use of QRC-160 pods. MiGs were now being vectored into position below the strike force at low altitudes, effectively making them invisible to US radar. They then climbed steeply to fire at the F-105s from below (or from above and to the rear, out of the US fighters' radar vision) in a single pass, before escaping at high speed, sometimes to sanctuary airfields in China.

More re-attacks on the Bac Giang railway yards on 23 August involved 18 F-105s. The afternoon strike on the Yen Vien railway yards near Hanoi was undertaken by an even larger package of 45 F-105s and 12 8th TFW F-4D bombers, with a single Phantom II MiGCAP flight led by Col Robin Olds. The latter force was initially ambushed by a pair of MiG-21s as it progressed down 'Thud Ridge', the VPAF fighters climbing up from very low altitude after hiding in radar ground 'clutter'. Diving out of heavy overcast, the communist pilots fired 'Atolls' that destroyed two 555th TFS Phantom IIs. Two more of the squadron's F-4Ds were also shot down while bombing, and the day's total losses eventually amounted to seven aircraft and five crewmen killed (five were also captured). Col Olds was furious that there had been no notification in the frontline of the implementation of new VPAF tactics, although Seventh Air Force high command was apparently aware of them.

In return, the only US aerial victory was achieved by 34th TFS F-105D pilot 1Lt David B Waldrop III. His 'Crossbow' flight, led by Maj Billy R Givens, was armed with M117 bombs, and it succeeded in hitting its target despite the degeneration of most of the strike effort into a huge MiG melée. Waldrop's bomb/gunsight was inoperative too. He reconstructed the engagement afterwards;

'As I rolled to the right I looked down and saw two MiG-17s. One was on the tail of an F-105 at the time. I picked up one and broke in on him. I plugged in my afterburner, picked up a little speed, closed in and started hosing off my cannon at him. Shortly afterwards some fire shot out from his wingtips and about mid-way across the wing, and he started a slow roll over to his right. I pulled up because I didn't want him to blow up in front of me. I came back down and fired again. I was pretty close and could see the pilot sitting in the cockpit. The whole right side of the fuselage and wing started lighting up. Pretty soon I saw the pilot eject. I saw the airplane roll off and hit the ground.'

Lacking a gunsight, Waldrop had selected an AIM-9B as his weapon of choice. He soon acquired a good 'growl' from its seeker, but he could not be sure that the missile had found the MiG-17 rather than the heat signature of the Thunderchief ahead of the enemy fighter. Switching to the cannon instead, Waldrop made short work of the MiG. Indeed, Col Olds, who witnessed its demise, likened the engagement to 'a shark chasing a minnow'.

1Lt David B Waldrop's name was applied to the canopy of F-105D 61-0132 *Hanoi Special* for publicity shots after his double MiG kill mission in the jet on 23 August 1967. His second claim was subsequently dismissed (*USAF*)

CHAPTER FIVE

Having destroyed his first adversary, Waldrop went after two more. In a left roll at 7500 ft, he opened fire on one at a range of 3000 ft and saw the flashes of bullet hits as he closed to within a half-mile of the MiG-17. The VPAF pilot escaped into clouds, but Waldrop rolled inverted and picked up the enemy jet as it emerged 2000 ft ahead of him. He fired another 250 rounds, watching them work back from the canopy to the tail, until the jet exploded and rolled inverted into the ground. Waldrop then exited the area.

During the same engagement 'Crossbow 1' (Givens) also took on a MiG that had damaged an F-105. He almost emptied his ammunition drum at it and claimed a probable kill. The 388th TFW's Enemy Aircraft Claims Board, having examined gun camera film, evidence from other pilots and general mission reports, validated both of Waldrop's claims and Givens' 'probable' kill. However, the Seventh Air Force Claims Board later dismissed Waldrop's second kill and Givens' claim.

Despite the success of this surprise attack on 23 August, the MiG units did not try their luck again for two months after MiGCAP cover was restored to its previous levels. The 8th TFW provided most of the CAP flights for the 355th TFW, while the 366th TFW escorted many of Korat's strikes.

By the early autumn the MiG-21s had returned with renewed vigour, shooting down two F-105s and prompting a strike on Phuc Yen airfield on 24 October. Six days earlier, during an afternoon strike on the Dai Loi railway bridge (a key crossing on the supply route from China), MiG-17s had engaged three of the four strike flights and the MiGCAP. Maj Donald M Russell was 'Wildcat 4', and his flight delivered its bombs successfully and then began to re-join as they exited the target area. He subsequently reported;

'MiGs had been seen in the target area just prior to roll-in. After about 180 degrees of turn I saw a MiG-17 crossing from my left approximately 1500 ft to 2000 ft out. I came

Hanoi Special (61-0132) loaded with M117s and an AIM-9B at Korat in June 1967. Some F-105s (including this aircraft) had a strike camera mounted beside the AN/APR-25/26 RHAW housing, beneath the nose of the jet, rather than behind it so that they could take photographs looking forward. In the background is another MiG killer, 60-0424 *Miss Carriage*, which was also christened *Mickey Titty Chi* (*Terry Panopalis collection*)

Capt Gene I Basel lies in traction in Korat hospital after his shoot-down by ground fire in February 1968, while his 354th TFS commander, Lt Col Jensen (accompanied by the entire squadron, who are out of shot to the left) awards him the Purple Heart, which he pinned on Basel's pillow. His other gift was a patch which read *78½ F-105 Missions North Vietnam*, a tour that included a MiG kill on 27 October 1967 (*USAF*)

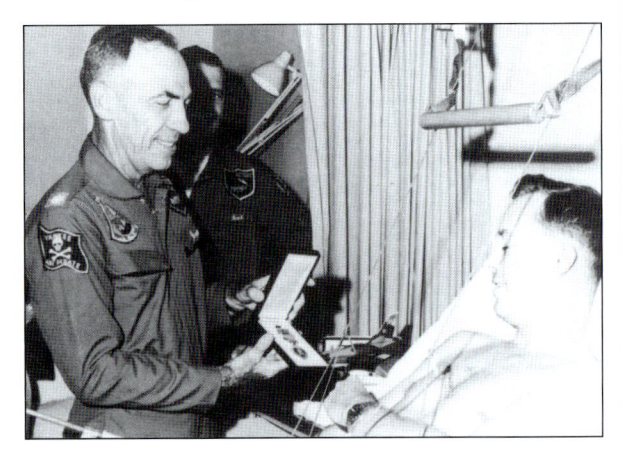

out of afterburner, extended the speed brakes and manoeuvred to his "six o'clock" position. He rolled out of his right turn and started a slow left turn to position himself behind a preceding F-105. His turn helped me to get into a good firing position and I opened fire at an estimated 1000 ft. I noticed flames from both sides of the MiG-17 aft of the cockpit area. I followed him for a few minutes and saw the fire increase. The aircraft rolled right and headed straight down. I did not see the pilot eject and lost sight of him at about 2000 ft going straight down in flames.'

Reconnaissance indicated that nine MiGs were destroyed on the ground in the 24 October Phuc Yen attack, reinforcing many pilots' belief that airfield bombing was the best, though long-delayed, way to dispose of enemy fighters. However, cratered runways were soon repaired and aircraft quickly replaced from Chinese and Soviet stocks, or assembled from crated parts stored near Phuc Yen. Indeed, more MiG-21s were supplied later in 1967, relegating MiG-17s to localised defence duties. Phuc Yen was active again on 26 October, but it lost three more MiG-17s to a flight of F-4Ds that day, and another to the 355th TFW 24 hours later.

The assault on Hanoi's transportation network continued, and the target on 27 October was the Canal des Rapides bridge. 'Bison' flight had been reduced to two aircraft by a flight control problem with the No 4 aircraft, and 'Bison Lead' (Maj Charles 'Ed' Cappelli) elected to join up with a flak suppression flight to maintain pod formation. There was an unprecedented number of SAMs fired at the strike force, and the *Wild Weasel* flight had used all of its Shrikes in killing three sites. Col John Flynn, vice-commander of the 388th TFW was hit by an SA-2 and became the highest-ranking prisoner-of-war at that time. 'Bison' bombed through a storm of 85 mm flak and pulled up off target, jinking violently. Capt Gene Basel ('Bison 2') found himself behind the rest of the flight and he suddenly noticed two MiG-17s ahead of him – his first sighting of an enemy fighter, and 'a perfect set-up for a high-speed pass'. He focused on one of the green-camouflaged MiGs;

'I closed to within 2000 ft, pulling lead on him. He didn't see me and was intent on positioning for an attack on the flight in front of me, until he felt the 20 mm impacts. At that time he reversed his direction abruptly, fire belching from his tailpipe. The MiG continued rolling left in an inverted position until it was lost from sight.'

Two of the MiG kill markings displayed on F-105D 62-4284 were for Capt Max Brestel's combat successes on 10 March 1967, and the third was added after Capt G I Basel's kill on 27 October that same year (*USAF*)

A 'boomer's' view of F-105D 62-4284 *Mary Kay*, with kill markings for Brestel and Basel, although only one appears on a white background (*Terry Panopalis collection*)

1Lt Cal W Tax, flying at the rear of the following F-105 flight, saw the MiG's wing tanks fall away and more flame streaming from the aircraft's tailpipe, indicating a fuel fire rather than normal afterburner. Basel's gun camera film confirmed that the MiG could not have recovered. He almost felled a second MiG during a subsequent attack on Kep that was resisted by numerous VPAF fighters, but he had to break off to avoid cannon rounds from a third MiG behind him and because SAM warnings had also been issued.

Another Kep attack on 3 November stirred up considerable MiG activity when the 355th TFW made the 800-mile trip to the VPAF base. Capt Wayne Warner ('Wolf 3'), on only his sixth mission, found himself close behind a MiG-17 over the airfield. In the heat of the moment he could not recall the complex gunsight procedure and started cranking in an appropriate depression angle manually. He engaged 'burner (but neglected to jettison his wing tanks) as he closed on the MiG, which was about to fire on another Thunderchief ahead of them. Uncertain at the last moment that it was indeed a MiG in his sights, Warner instinctively looked behind him and found two more MiGs on his tail, which he managed to lose through some strenuous manoeuvring.

MiG-KILLING SAM SLAYERS

The last two confirmed MiG-17 kills achieved by the Thunderchief occurred on the same day, and both were credited to F-105F *Iron Hand* crews from 'Otter' flight of the 355th TFW, bringing the Takhli wing's final total to 19.5 victories. A third MiG-17 was claimed by the flight lead at the time, but subsequently disallowed.

December 1967 brought another change in VPAF tactics, with MiG-17s and MiG-21s working together to make coordinated multiple passes from different directions rather than single 'hit and run' assaults. These tactics were used by ten MiGs to force the first wave of F-105s on the 19 December attack on Viet Tri and Tien Cuong to jettison their bombs. The USAF modified its tactics successfully too, allowing a wider time gap between the two attack waves so that the MiGs would concentrate on the first wave and then have to land to refuel, at which point the second formation would carry out its attacks.

One of the MiG-17s shot down on 19 December was jointly claimed by a MiGCAP Phantom II crew (Maj Joseph Moore and 1Lt George McKinney Jnr) and Majs William M Dalton and James L Graham from the F-105F *Iron Hand* flight near Phuc Yen. Weapons Systems Officer George McKinney described the first part of the encounter to the author;

'Our CAP flight ["Nash"] was just joining up with the F-105s near the "elbow" in the Black River when the "Thuds" were jumped by a large number of MiG-17s. To put it mildly, a giant "furball" ensued. All types of aircraft were going every which way, there were missiles in the air and bombs

The story behind this famous image may be less familiar. F-105D 60-5376 *Rum Runner/Excedrin Headache* was 'Locust 2', with Lt Col Rufus Dye at the controls, in a 388th TFW strike on Thong Quang railway yard on 7 November 1967. Near the target two MiG-21s appeared and fired 'Atolls' at the lead flight. The first missed, but a missile from the second aircraft overshot its target and hit Dye's aircraft in the second flight. It exploded inside the tail and debris tore into the rear fuselage, knocking out the utility hydraulics, drag 'chute and airbrakes. Despite lacking an afterburner, Dye still obtained full military power from the tough J75 engine and 'force refuelled' from a tanker by asking its pilot to 'toboggan' in a shallow dive. Without hydraulics to lock the refuelling boom into his aircraft's receptacle, Dye kept the boom in place by using engine thrust. Utilising his emergency systems, he recovered safely to Udorn RTAFB. The aircraft was repaired and continued in service until 1977. Korat pilots were shown this photo as a morale booster (*USAF*)

Lt Gen Benjamin Davis, commander of the Thirteenth Air Force, awards the Silver Star to Maj William Wheeler (357th TFS) following his 19 December 1967 MiG kill (*HQ Seventh Air Force/USAF*)

F-105F 63-8317 was flown by Capt Drew and Maj Wheeler during their MiG-17 engagement on 19 December 1967. Nicknamed *Half Fast*, it carries an AGM-45A/B Shrike on its outer underwing pylon for its vital anti-SAM role (*USAF*)

and tanks were being hastily jettisoned. In the midst of this "fog of war" Maj Moore spotted a MiG-17 approximately three miles ahead at our "12 o'clock" and I obtained a radar lock-on [for their AIM-7 missiles].

'As we were closing to maximum AIM-7 range an F-105 with a MiG-17 in hot pursuit flew directly across our flightpath about a mile in front. Immediately forsaking what appeared to be a sure kill, Joe turned hard right to help the "Thud". They were in a descending right turn. Maj Moore skilfully arced the circle, performed a beautiful left barrel roll and obtained a moderate deflection gun shot at the MiG from about 1500 yards. I saw at least two 'sparkles' from the MiG's aft fuselage, whereupon he seemed to relax all Gs and trail wispy, white smoke.'

This was McKinney's third successful engagement using the SUU-23/A gun pod beneath the F-4D, which, although less accurate than the F-105's gun installation, gave the same close-in, lacerating rate of fire. As he put it, with 2.5 kills chalked up, 'That's how I became the only "half ace" of the Vietnam War'. The other half of the victory was awarded to the crew of 'Otter 2', commanded by Maj Dalton, who encountered the same MiG moments later, apparently intent upon attacking Maj Robert R Huntley and Capt Ralph W Stearman in 'Otter 1'. Maj Dalton explained how he began to slow down and turn right to get behind him;

'I closed as much as I could, started tracking and then fired. I fired a short burst but was not tracking him, so I let up on the trigger, repositioned the pipper ahead of the MiG and let him fly into it. I then tracked him again and opened fire. I observed impacts on the left wing and left side of the fuselage under the cockpit. I turned to follow him but he rolled and headed down inverted off to my left.'

This was all recorded on 'Otter 2's' gun camera, although the jet's final demise was missed on film as its crew had to break away as more MiGs were entering the fight. However, Maj Dalton did see two impact points on the ground 'which I assumed were downed MiGs'.

Capt Philip M Drew and Maj William H Wheeler, in 'Otter 3', also had two MiG-17s to contend with as they closed rapidly on the tail of their Thunderchief. Drew turned the big F-105F hard towards them and dived into a valley to gain airspeed;

'I picked up a MiG at my "one o'clock high" position heading in about the same direction as I was going. He appeared to be by himself. I was low on him, and I don't believe he ever saw me. As he started a gentle right turn I started my attack, firing 756 rounds of 20 mm ammunition until I could see the ends of the MiG's wingtips on each side of my canopy bow, which put him about 100 ft away. I saw numerous rounds impacting his fuselage and his right wing-root area. As I crossed over the top of him I clearly saw the aircraft markings on top of the left wing.

'Maj Wheeler called that we had another MiG attacking us from our left. I picked out the new attacker about 1000 ft out at my "nine o'clock" with his guns ablaze. I looked back at my target one last time and saw him rolling into a 120-degree bank. Due to my position I could not see beyond the tail of the MiG I had fired on to observe the intensity of the smoke and fire. I was still close to him since I could now clearly see the red star on his fuselage. I then pushed over, obtained negative 2g and continued rolling to the left until I reached 50 ft above the ground and lost my attacker. I made a slow 360-degree turn back to the area, looking for more MiGs, and to pick up my wingman, and I saw black and grey smoke mushrooming up where an aircraft had impacted the ground. This coincided exactly with the direction and attitude of flight of my MiG.'

'Otter 1' (Maj Huntley and Capt Stearman) thought they had destroyed a MiG too, but their claim was turned down after two years due to lack of conclusive evidence from witnesses or gun camera film, although the latter clearly showed the aircraft on fire. In Maj Huntley's report he described how he had 'pulled hard into a left climbing turn to establish a head-on firing pass. As I was climbing through approximately 2500 ft I fired at the MiG while still in a head-on pass. I observed my 20 mm HEI [high-explosive incendiary ammunition] impacting in the fuselage area and saw him start trailing heavy black smoke. At no time did he attempt to roll out of his bank angle or pull out of a dive. Suddenly, my peripheral vision caught another MiG trailing black smoke in a spiral dive approximately one mile south of the MiG I had shot at. I was unable to see the disabled MiG impact the ground'.

Huntley and Stearman were flying F-105F 63-8320, which eventually had three MiG kills marked up on its nose. One of these apparently originated from the belief that Drew and Wheeler were flying this aircraft (rather than 63-8317) on 19 December.

The prescriptive rules for awarding MiG kills ruled out a number of other claims that might have passed if gun cameras had been more reliable and other flight members had seen the demise of enemy fighters more clearly through the confusion of combat.

Operation *Rolling Thunder* continued until 1 November 1968, but MiG activity had reduced significantly from 31 March as President Johnson progressively moved the 'bombing line' further south, restricting attacks on the North to the point where most of North Vietnam was a 'MiG sanctuary'. Indeed, the last USAF MiG kill during the campaign

F-105F/G 63-8320, one of the best-known F-105s, wore three MiG kills below its cockpit for most of its long career, including post-war 35th TFW service. In fact the MiG kills were all unconfirmed, despite gun camera evidence of hits and fire damage on a MiG-17 by Maj Robert Huntley and Capt Ralph Stearman ('Otter 1'). In the same *Iron Hand* flight were Drew and Wheeler ('Otter 3') and Dalton and Graham ('Otter 2'). Both these crews were awarded kills, and one of the stars on 63-8320 originates from the belief that Dalton/Graham were flying this aircraft rather than 63-8329. The third star has more bizarre origins. Maj George O Guss (333rd TFS) was wingman in a two-ship flight on his first North Vietnam mission in 1967 when he was jumped by four MiG-17s that advanced behind and below him. Guss pressed the 'master panic button', jettisoning his bombs, rocket pods and pylons. Moments later the F-105 flight leader saw a ball of fire behind him and an aircraft heading downwards. Guss was convinced that a MiG had flown into his falling ordnance, but there was insufficient evidence to support the claim (*Author's collection*)

Capt Philip M Drew piloted F-105F 63-8317 in which he and Maj Wheeler downed a MiG-17. His Silver Star was awarded to him by Maj Gen Kenneth Dempster, Thirteenth Air Force vice-commander (*HQ Seventh Air Force/USAF*)

(by a Phantom II crew) occurred on 14 February, as MiGs hardly ever ventured south of the bombing line to challenge US air operations. Nevertheless, the first six weeks of 1968 saw extensive aerial combat resulting in eight MiG kills, although none by F-105 crews. This was primarily because the number of F-4 MiGCAP flights had increased while Thunderchief strike flights had been reduced. Three of the 34 F-105s lost in 1968 were downed by MiGs, the last of these occurring on 4 February. VPAF pilots claimed no more Thunderchiefs until 11 May 1972, when an F-105G *Wild Weasel* was destroyed over Hanoi.

F-105D/F operations shifted to Laos with the end of *Rolling Thunder*. The jet's high speed was no real advantage in the new area of conflict, and the Phantom II could carry more bombs with a twin-engine safety factor. The introduction of the gun-armed F-4E, together with a significant reduction in the F-105 force due to attrition (393 were lost to all causes in Southeast Asia, and with production having ended in January 1965, there were no replacements available) impelled the transition of the 388th TFW at Korat to the F-4E in late 1969. The wing's F-105F *Wild Weasel* unit (44th TFS) was reassigned to Takhli in November of that year, and F-105D operations ceased at the Thai air base on 10 October 1970.

From the beginning of October 1967 until the end of *Rolling Thunder*, USAF fighters could claim 27 MiG kills for the loss of 24 aircraft to VPAF fighters, 16 of them to MiG-21s. Only five MiG-21s were shot down in return. The VPAF had become a well-coordinated force that had learned to make the most of its geographical advantages, and devised tactics that enabled it to cope with superior American technology. The standard of pilot training also improved, with some individuals having fought from the beginning of the war. As they gained combat experience they passed this on to younger recruits.

F-105 pilots, on the other hand, seldom remained in-theatre longer than their single 100-mission tours. Many pilots came to the battle with little experience of air-to-air combat. In that context, the Thunderchief crews' 22 kills in 1967, four of them during that challenging final quarter, reflect great credit on the F-105 pilots and their comparatively unsophisticated air combat capability. For them, their victories over MiGs were a more obvious token of success in the war than the often uncertain achievements from attacking targets that seemed to have little strategic value, in circumstances which made many of them adopt the motto 'Ain't no way' after experiencing missions in Route Pack VI. They also clearly demonstrated their versatility (and that of the F-105) by achieving success in situations that they were not originally trained to encounter.

APPENDICES

F-105 THUNDERCHIEF MiG KILLERS

All VPAF aircraft involved were MiG-17s. All USAF aircraft are F-105Ds unless shown with * to indicate an F-105F. In several cases serial numbers of the relevant Thunderchiefs were not recorded, or are uncertain, as explained in the notes for the Colour Plates. Several other possible and unconfirmed kills are described within the text. Finally, Majs Dalton and Graham shared their MiG-17 with an F-4D Phantom II crew ('Nash 1') from the 435th TFS/8th TFW. Maj Joseph D Moore (pilot) and 1Lt George H McKinney Jnr (WSO) had already damaged the MiG with 20 mm gunfire.

1966

Date	Serial/Call sign	Crew	Unit	Weapon
29 June	58-1156/'Crab 2'	Maj Fred L Tracy	421st TFS/388th TFW	20 mm
18 August	60-0458/'Honda 2'	Maj Kenneth T Blank	34th TFS/388th TFW	20 mm
21 September	59-1766/'Ford 3'	1Lt Karl W Richter	421st TFS/388th TFW	20 mm
21 September	unknown/'Vegas 2'	1Lt Fred A Wilson	333rd TFS/355th TFW	20 mm
4 December	62-4278/'Elgin 4'	Maj Roy S Dickey	469th TFS/388th TFW	20 mm

1967

Date	Serial/Call sign	Crew	Unit	Weapon
10 March	62-4284/'Kangaroo 3'	Capt Max C Brestel	354 TFS/355th TFW	20 mm (two kills)
26 March	59-1772/'Leech 1'	Col Robert R Scott	333rd TFS/355th TFW	20 mm
19 April	63-8301*/'Kingfish 1'	Maj Leo K Thorsness (pilot)	357th TFS/355th TFW	20 mm
19 April	63-8301*/'Kingfish 1'	Capt Harold E Johnson (EWO)	357th TFS/355th TFW	20 mm
19 April	58-1168/'Nitro 1'	Maj Jack W Hunt	354th TFS/355th TFW	20 mm
19 April	62-4364/'Panda 1'	Capt William E Eskew	354th TFS/355th TFW	20 mm
19 April	62-4384/'Nitro 3'	Maj Frederick G Tolman	354th TFS/355th TFW	20 mm
28 April	59-1772/'Spitfire 1'	Maj Harry E Higgins	357th TFS/355th TFW	20 mm
28 April	60-0504/'Atlanta 1'	Lt Col Arthur F Dennis	357th TFS/355th TFW	20 mm
30 April	60-0498/'Rattler 1'	Capt Thomas C Lesan	333rd TFS/355th TFW	20 mm
12 May	61-0159/'Crossbow 1'	Capt Jacques Suzanne	333rd TFS/355th TFW	20 mm
13 May	unknown/'Chevrolet 3'	Capt Charles W Couch	354th TFS/355th TFW	20 mm
13 May	60-0501/'Chevrolet 1'	Lt Col Philip C Gast	354th TFS/355th TFW	20 mm
13 May	60-0497/'Kimona 2'	Maj Maurice E Seaver Jnr	44th TFS/388th TFW	20 mm
13 May	60-0522/'Random 1'	Maj Robert G Rilling	333rd TFS/355th TFW	AIM-9B
13 May	62-4262/'Random 3'	Maj Carl D Osborne	333rd TFS/355th TFW	AIM-9B
3 June	60-0424/'Hambone 2'	Maj Ralph L Kuster Jnr	13th TFS/388th TFW	20 mm
3 June	61-0069/'Hambone 3'	Capt Larry D Wiggins	469th TFS/388th TFW	20 mm/AIM-9B
23 August	61-0132/'Crossbow 3'	1Lt David B Waldrop III	34th TFS/388th TFW	20 mm
18 October	62-4394/'Wildcat 4'	Maj Donald M Russell	333rd TFS/355th TFW	20 mm
27 October	62-4284/'Bison 2'	Capt Gene I Basel	354th TFS/355th TFW	20 mm
19 December	63-8329*/'Otter 2'	Maj William M Dalton (pilot)	333rd TFS/355th TFW	20 mm
19 December	63-8329*/'Otter 2'	Maj James M Graham (EWO)	333rd TFS/355th TFW	20 mm
19 December	63-8317*/'Otter 3'	Capt Philip M Drew (pilot)	357th TFS/355th TFW	20 mm
19 December	63-8317*/'Otter 3'	Maj William H Wheeler (EWO)	357th TFS/355th TFW	20 mm

COLOUR PLATES

1
F-105D-5-RE 58-1156 of the 421st TFS/388th TFW, Korat RTAFB, Thailand, 29 June 1966

Maj Fred Tracy probably flew this 'reverse camouflage' (areas of 30219 Tan and 34102 Green were reversed on some aircraft) as 'Crab 02' in an *Iron Hand* mission that resulted in the first F-105 MiG kill. The MiG star denoting this victory was evident when MiG killer Karl Richter flew his 100th mission in 58-1156 – Richter's victory had come in 59-1766. Tracy's aircraft is depicted here carrying LAU-3/A rocket pods. On 21 January 1967 58-1156 crashed 50 miles off the coast of North Vietnam after it had been hit by a large calibre AAA shell during an attack on rail targets around Kep. Although seriously injured ejecting from the aircraft, Capt W R Wyatt was rescued by a US Navy helicopter.

2
F-105D-31-RE 62-4278 of the 469th TFS/388th TFW, Korat RTAFB, Thailand, 4 December 1966

Probably flown by Maj Roy S Dickey as 'Elgin 04' (some records cite 60-0518 as Dickey's mount), this aircraft was loaded with six M117 bombs and two QRC-160 ECM pods. Dickey downed a MiG-17 as the F-105s came off their target. 62-4278 was destroyed by AAA on 12 August 1967 during an attack on the Paul Doumer Bridge, its pilot, Capt T E Norris, being captured.

3
F-105D-20-RE 61-0109 of the 355th TFW, Takhli RTAFB, Thailand, May 1967

This aircraft was issued to Col Robert R Scott, CO of the 355th TFW, after his original jet, 61-0105, was lost (much to his annoyance) to AAA on 8 May 1967. It was also used by his successor, Col John C Giraudo, who christened it the *Big Kahuna*. 61-0109's MiG kill (marked up beneath the cockpit) was transferred from F-105D 59-1772, which Col Scott had used to shoot down a MiG-17 on 26 March 1967. Scott's name appeared both on the canopy frame and on the nose-gear door of 61-0109.

4
F-105F-1-RE 63-8301 of the 357th TFS/355th TFW, Takhli RTAFB, Thailand, 19 April 1967

Maj Leo Thorsness and Capt Harold E Johnson led 'Kingfish' flight in this jet on 19 April 1967, the aircraft being loaded with CBU-24 canisters, AGM-45 Shrike missiles and QRC-160 ECM pods. The flight faced three engagements with MiG-17s and 'Kingfish 1' shot one of them down. This F-105F crashed in peacetime service shortly before it could take its rightful place in the National Museum of the USAF at Wright-Patterson AFB, Ohio.

5
F-105D-31-RE 62-4364 of the 354th TFS/355th TFW, Takhli RTAFB, Thailand, 19 April 1967

Three more MiG-17s were shot down during aerial battles over the rescue effort for Majs Madison and Sterling ('Kingfish 2') on 19 April 1967, with the destruction of one of the VPAF fighters being credited to Capt William E 'Gene' Eskew in this F-105D. 62-4364 was subsequently written off after a 5 February 1969 ground accident.

6
F-105D-5-RE 58-1168, of the 354th TFS/355th TFW, Takhli RTAFB, Thailand, April 1967

Maj Jack Hunt downed a MiG-17 in the same dogfights as Eskew and Thorsness whilst leading 'Nitro' strike flight, which was configured with M117 bombs and QRC-160 pods, with AIM-9Bs for 'Nitro 1' and '3'. This reverse-camouflaged aircraft, which was later used by Hunt for his 100th mission, fell victim to AAA during a 25 October 1967 attack on the Paul Doumer Bridge. The pilot of the aircraft, Maj R E Smith, was captured.

7
F-105D-31-RE 62-4384 of the 354th TFS/355th TFW, Takhli RTAFB, Thailand, 19 April 1967

Another MiG-17 fell to 'Nitro' flight via Maj Fred Tolman's M61A1 gun. Tolman was also flying this F-105D when he accidentally strafed the Russian freighter *Turkestan* in Cam Pha harbour on 2 June 1967 after his flight had taken ground fire from positions around the ship. The incident ended his USAF career after a punitive court martial.

8
F-105D-6-RE 59-1772 of the 357th TFS/355th TFW, Takhli RTAFB, Thailand, 28 April 1967

With victory symbols beneath its cockpit for MiGs downed by Col Robert Scott and Maj Harry E Higgins, this aircraft (coded RK by August 1967) also bears evidence of use by 333rd TFS 'Lancers' commander Lt Col Bill Norris with *No 1 Lancer* titling again below the cockpit. Higgins' assigned F-105D featured an *Andy Capp* figure painted on its nose. 59-1772 was yet another ground fire casualty, being brought down on a *Barrel Roll* mission over northern Laos on 27 January 1970. Maj D W Livingston ejected from the aircraft and was rescued by a USAF HH-53C helicopter.

9
F-105D-10-RE 60-0498 of the 333rd TFS/355th TFW, Takhli RTAFB, Thailand, 30 April 1967

On a day when three F-105s were lost to enemy action Capt Thomas C Lesan downed a MiG-17 with 20 mm gunfire during a strike mission with M117 bombs. The original low-visibility black serials on USAF tactical aircraft were modified in 1967 to include white numerals. Variously nicknamed *Boobs* and *Top Dog*, 60-0498 ended its days serving with the Virginia Air National Guard.

10
F-105D-20-RE 61-0159 of the 333rd TFS/355th TFW, Takhli RTAFB, Thailand, 12 May 1967

As 'Crossbow' strike flight lead, carrying 750-lb bombs, Capt Jacques Suzanne brought down a MiG-17 with 20 mm fire. The VPAF fighters were menacing 'Warhawk' flight, ahead of 'Crossbow', which in turn made them vulnerable to Suzanne's flight.

11
F-105D-20-RE 61-0136 of the 354th TFS/355th TFW, Takhli RTAFB, Thailand, May 1967
This aircraft was assigned to Capt Charles W Couch, although it was possibly not the MiG killer he flew on 13 May 1967 as the tail number of his assigned F-105D that day was not recorded. Couch was part of Lt Col Gast's 'Chevrolet' strike flight, with 750-lb bombs and an AIM-9. However, this illustration shows the jet with Mk 82 500-lb bombs and an AGM-45 Shrike missile – a typical configuration for a SAM suppression sortie.

12
F-105D-30-RE 62-4262 of the 333rd TFS/355th TFW, Takhli RTAFB, 13 May 1967
Maj Carl D Osborne, as 'Random 3', was another participant in the major dogfights of 13 May 1967. He and his flight leader, Maj Robert Rilling, both destroyed MiG-17s with AIM-9Bs. This aircraft, also used for Maj Osborne's 105th mission in July 1967, bore the nickname *Duck* and RK tail codes by the time it was brought down by an 85 mm AAA shell whilst attacking Kep airfield on 24 October 1967. Its pilot, Capt M D Scott, was rescued by a US Navy helicopter.

13
F-105D-10-RE 60-0497 of the 44th TFS/388th TFW, Korat RTAFB, Thailand, May 1967
Another MiG-17 fell to Maj Maurice E 'Mo' Seaver's 'Tamale' flight lead aircraft *Miss T* on 13 May. With his aircraft armed with M117 bombs and carrying QRC-160 pods, Seaver detected a camouflaged MiG-17 ahead of his flight and swiftly felled it with 20 mm gunfire. 60-0497 was in turn shot down by a MiG-21 near Phuc Yen airfield on 18 November 1967, the aircraft being one of four F-105s lost during this mission. Lt Col W N Reed ejected from the stricken jet after coaxing it into neighbouring Laos, the pilot being rescued by a USAF helicopter.

14
F-105D-6-RE 60-0424 of the 13th TFS/388th TFW, Korat RTAFB, Thailand, 3 June 1967
Armed with M118 bombs, 'Hambone' flight hit the Bac Giang Bridge on 3 June 1967. Maj Ralph L Kuster Jnr, as 'Hambone 2', fired three bursts of 20 mm rounds at a MiG-17, blowing off its wing. His F-105D, *Mickey Titty Chi*, was lost to AAA on 10 July 1967. Its pilot, MiG killer Maj 'Mo' Seaver, ejected safely from the stricken jet and was rescued by a USAF HH-3 helicopter.

15
F-105D-15RE 61-0069 of the 469th TFS/388th TFW, Korat RTAFB, Thailand, 3 June 1967
Capt Larry D Wiggins was 'Hambone 3' on the 3 June 1967 mission. His single AIM-9B damaged a MiG-17, which he then destroyed with 20 mm gunfire. This aircraft later moved to the 355th TFW, where it was nicknamed *Pussy Galore* and then *Cherry Girl* and adorned with some infamously suggestive artwork.

16
F-105D-20-RE 61-0132 of the 34th TFS/338th TFW, Korat RTAFB, Thailand, 23 August 1967
1Lt David B Waldrop was 'Crossbow 3' in a strike flight targeting the Yen Vien railway yard when he shot down a MiG-17 and also had a brief opportunity to fire at a MiG-21 before it accelerated away. His gun camera film revealed an F-105 passing between him and the MiG-17 while he was firing, with flames coming from the Thunderchief. When 61-0132 was subsequently coded 'JJ' its *Hanoi Special* artwork just below the engine intake was modified.

17
F-105D-31-RE 62-4284 of the 453th TFS/355th TFW, Takhli RTAFB, Thailand, 27 October 1967
Capt Gene I Basel flew this Thunderchief, armed with two 3000-lb M118 bombs, as 'Bison 2' for an attack on the Canal des Rapides Bridge on 27 October 1967 that resulted in the destruction of three USAF aircraft, and a MiG kill for Basel. It already wore two victory stars for Capt Max Brestel's MiG victories on 10 March 1967. Having survived the war, 62-4284 crashed during a training mission near Clayton, Oklahoma, on 12 March 1976, killing Capt Larry L Klein.

18
F-105F-1-RE 63-8329 of the 333rd TFS/355th TFW, Takhli RTAFB, Thailand, 19 December 1967
Majs William M Dalton and James M Graham were 'Otter 2' in a SAM suppression role on 19 December 1967 when they shared in the destruction of a MiG-17 with an 8th TFW crew. 63-8329, thought to have been their F-105F that day, was nicknamed *Rosemary's Baby*, *The Protestor's Protector* and *My Diane*. It was lost to AAA on 28 January 1970, and an HH-53 'Jolly Green' helicopter attempting to rescue the crew of the Thunderchief was shot down shortly thereafter by a MiG-21. Capts R J Mallon and R J Panek ejected successfully but were reportedly executed by North Vietnamese militia shortly after their capture.

19
F-105F-1-RE 63-8317 of the 357th TFS/355th TFW, Takhli RTAFB, Thailand, 19 December 1967
'Otter' *Iron Hand* flight claimed two MiG-17s on 19 December 1967 and the flight leader, Maj Robert Huntley, damaged a third. Capt Phillip M Drew and Maj William H Wheeler, in 63-8317 *Half Fast*, closed to within 100 ft of a MiG-17 to ensure its destruction with 20 mm gunfire.

20
F-105D-6-RE 60-0415 of the 354th TFS/355th TFW, Takhli RTAFB, Thailand, April 1967
Identifying MiG killer F-105s has been made more complicated over the years by the pilots' (and groundcrews') tradition of transferring victory markings to other aircraft assigned to them, or marking up claimed kills that were later disallowed. This jet, *Honey Brown*, recorded an unidentified kill beneath its cockpit on the left side of the fuselage.

21
F-105D-10-RE 60-0522 of the 333rd TFS/355th TFW Takhli RTAFB, Thailand, April 1968
At the time of Maj Robert G Rilling's MiG encounter on 13 May 1967, this Thunderchief displayed its identity in six-inch white characters (*USAF 00522*) on its tail. Tail code usage was resisted by the 355th TFW wing commander, Col Bob Scott, but a few examples appeared after he left Takhli in August 1967. However, all MiG killer F-105s were almost certainly un-coded at the time of their dogfights. Rilling's MiG kill accounts for only one of the two stars that appeared beneath the cockpit of 60-0522 by April 1968, the circumstances surrounding the second marking remaining unrecorded.

22
F-105D-31-RE 62-4394 of the 333rd TFS/355th TFW, Takhli RTAFB, Thailand, 1968

This aircraft also carried two kill markings, one of them for Maj Donald M Russell's MiG-17, which he claimed on 18 October 1967. It was later assigned to Col John C Giraudo, commander of the 355th TFW, on 2 August 1967 and adorned with his nickname, the *Big Kahuna*.

23
F-105D-10-RE 60-0504 of the 357th TFS/355th TFW, Takhli RTAFB, Thailand, 1968

Flying as 'Atlanta 1', Lt Col Arthur F Dennis used this aircraft to claim a MiG-17 kill on 28 April 1967. The following month Capt Thomas Lesan recorded an unconfirmed MiG kill in the same jet, hence the two red stars beneath the cockpit. Re-assigned to Maj Buddy Jones in 1968 and tail-coded, 60-0504 was nicknamed *Memphis Belle II* and subsequently displayed at the National Museum of the USAF at Wright-Patterson AFB.

24
F-105D-31-RE 62-4284 of the 354th TFS/355th TFW, Takhli RTAFB, Thailand, 1968

By the time it was tail-coded in 1968 this F-105D bore three kill markings. One was for Capt Gene Basel's October 1967 victory and the remaining two were derived from a double MiG kill on 10 March 1967 by Capt Max C Brestel, who was flying as 'Kangaroo 3' in a strike on the Thai Nguyen steel mill. Configured for flak suppression, it carried four CBU-24 canisters, an AIM-9B and a QRC-160 ECM pod that day.

25
F-105D-10-RE 60-0458 of the 34th TFS/388th TFW, Korat RTAFB, Thailand, July 1969

This aircraft, tail-coded in 1968, is shown with the same type of CBU-3/A ordnance that it carried as 'Honda 2' on 18 August 1967 when Maj Kenneth T Blank shot down a MiG-17 with 20 mm gunfire during an *Iron Hand* sortie.

26
F-105D-6-RE 59-1766 of the Test, Research and Development Division, 4520th Combat Crew Training Wing, Nellis AFB, Nevada, 22 September 1962

Seen near the beginning of its service career, this F-105D, like most others, was called to war and joined the 421st TFS/388th TFW. It was 1Lt Karl Richter's aircraft ('Ford 3') on 21 September 1966 for his MiG kill. The jet survived until 28 February 1967, when it was brought down by AAA near the hazardous Mu Gia Pass. Its pilot, Capt J S Walbridge, was rescued by a USAF HH-3E helicopter.

27
F-105D-10-RE 60-0501 of the 36th TFW, Bitburg AB, West Germany, 1962

Another MiG killer F-105D in more colourful decor early in its career, this example was reassigned to the 354th TFS/355th TFW. The aircraft was subsequently flown by Lt Col Phillip C Gast for his 13 May 1967 MiG kill mission. In 1962 'Thuds' still had weather-prone natural metal finish and lacked ECM equipment, strike cameras, 'dog-ear' rear fuselage air intakes and a revised intake at the base of the fin – all modifications that were synonymous with examples based in Thailand from 1965.

28
F-105D-20-RE 61-0159 of the 149th TFS/192nd TFG, Virginia ANG, Byrd ANGB, Virginia, 1980

One of a handful of MiG killer F-105s that survived the war to see service with the Air National Guard, this example was the mount of Capt Jacques A Suzanne ('Crossbow 1') on 12 May 1967 when it carried M117 bombs, an AIM-9B and a QRC-160 pod, with two 450-gallon wing tanks. Note the victory star on the wing leading edge and the fighter's nickname, *HAVE GUN WILL TRAVEL*, immediately below the wing.

29
F-105D-15-RE 61-0069 of the 466th TFS/508th TFG, Hill AFB, Utah, 1981

Previously flown by Capt Larry D Wiggins for his 3 June 1967 MiG kill, this aircraft still displayed the victory marking beneath the cockpit during its Air Force Reserve service with the 465th and 466th TFSs prior to the jet's well earned retirement to the San Bernardino County Museum from 1984 to January 2000. Following restoration, the aircraft has since been displayed within the Strategic Air Command Museum in Omaha, Nebraska. During 61-0069's single year in Thailand with the 388th TFW it was also flown by MiG killers Kuster, Seaver and Basel.

30
F-105D-31-RE 62-4301 of the 466th TFS/419th TFW, Hill AFB, Utah, 1983

In a distinctive camouflage scheme that represented TAC colours in the early 1980s, the well-known *My Karma* carried a prominent victory symbol in its latter days in October 1983. This derived from an Ilyushin Il-28 'ground kill' that was possibly transferred from another aircraft since 62-4301 spent only a few weeks at Takhli in 1966, before airfield attacks began. It was one of the last F-105Ds to fly, retiring to the McClellan Aviation Museum, in California, in January 1984.

INDEX

Note: locators in **bold** refer to illustrations, captions and plates.

'100 F-105 Missions over North Vietnam' flag **29**
100th mission 'dunking' **79**

acceleration 6, 15
afterburners and performance 14–15, 16, 17, 34, 37, 39, 44, 47, 68
air intake **80**
air-to-air training 21–22, 37, 48, 91

airplanes: EC-121 radar surveillance plane 38, 84; F-4 Phantom II fighter-bomber 9, 14, 16, 24, 25, **27**, 28, **34,** 39, 62, 84, 90–91; F-4C Phantom II 39–40, 41, 61, 62, 64, 69–70, 75, 76, 77, 80, 88, 91; F-8 Crusader fighter plane 50, 61; F-86H Sabre fighter plane 21; F-100D Super Sabre fighter-bomber 27, **27**; F-102A Delta Dagger interceptor plane 21; F-104C Starfighter fighter-bomber 27; MiG-17 fighter plane (USSR) 4, 14–15, **15**, 16, **17,** 17–18, 25, 26, 28, 29, 32, 34, 37, 42, 43, 46, 48, 50, 61, 62–63, 64–66, 68, 69, 70, 73, 75–76, 77, 85, 86–87, 88–90; MiG-17PF fighter plane (USSR) 35, 46; MiG-21 fighter plane (USSR) 14–15, **17,** 20, 25, 30, 31–32, 34, 38, 43, 44, 45–46, 49–50, 61, 65, 75, 86, 87, 88
Allinson, Capt David J. 35, 62
ambush spots **15**
ammunition feed 10–11
armament loading **13,** 50
armament switches 45, 63

INDEX

attacks on transportation networks 22, 62, 75, 87, **88**
Australian bush hats **66**

BARCAP (barrier combat air patrol) missions 27
barrel changes 12
Basel, Capt Gene I. **7,** 24, **83, 86, 87,** 87–88
Blank, Maj Kenneth T **37**
bombs: CBU-24 canister cluster bombs 44, 62, 65, 66, 74, 75; M117 70, 77; M118 3049-lb bomb **30,** 31, 39, **47,** 73, 81
Boyd, Col John 16, 23, 40
Brestel, Capt Max C. **7,** 62–63, **63, 87**
Broughton, Col Jack 13–14, 20, 49, **63,** 76
Brucher, Capt John **22**

camouflage **7, 15, 22, 27,** 31, **68,** 78, **81**
CAP (combat air patrol) missions 24, 25, 27, **27,** 76, 88
close-in firing 76
cockpit of F-105D **18**
communications problems 33, 34, 47, 62
'Crab' mission of USAF TFS 28–29
crowded radio frequencies 33

Dap Cau missions 38, 39, 41–42, 43
defence cuts 9, **11o**
Dennis, Col Arthur **65,** 74, **74**
design 6–10, 18, 26
development 6
Dickey, Maj Roy S. 48, **48,** 49
dogfight tactics **39, 49**
dogfights 4, 15–17, 20, 23, 26, 29, 32, 33–35, 38, 40–42, 45–50, 62–63, 71–72, 76, 77, 79–80, 81, 82–83, 85–90
Drew, Capt Philip M. **91**

fire-control system 9
flak suppression flights 44, 62–63, 73, 74, 76, 77, 87
flight formations 16, 19, 21, 22, 24, 25, **25,** 44-45, 81
Flynn, Col John **7**
fuel capacity 17

Gast, Lt Gen Philip C 62, **62,** 63, 78
GCI (ground-controlled interception) 27, 38, 72
gun cameras **28,** 35, **39,** 40, 48, 68, 69, 72, 74, 78, 81, **83, 86,** 88, 89, 90, **90**
gun platform difficulties **18,** 18–19
gunsight problems 37, 41, 48, 62, 63, 69, 74, 85, 88

Han Phong mission 73–75
Higgins, Maj Harry E 'Hank' 73–74
Hunt, Maj Jack W **67,** 67–68, 69
Huntley, Maj Robert 90, **91**

in-flight refuelling **35, 70,** 70–71
initial combat 22–23
Iron Hand missions 26, 28, 30, **30,** 31–32, 36, 38, 40, 41, 49, 63, 65, 72, 88–90, **90**

jammed guns 37, 40, 42, 61, 62, 73
jettisoning of ordnance 4, **25,** 25–26, 31, 32, 34, 40, 41, 42, 43, **43,** 48, 49, 50, 61, 70, **81,** 88–89, **90**
Johnson, President Lyndon 28, 64, 90

Kasler, Maj Jim 12, 33, 34, 62
kills 24, 25, 27–28, 48, 72, 77, 78, **80,** 85–86, 88, **89,** 90, **90,** 91, **92**
Kriz, Maj William J **21**
Kuster, Maj Ralph 81-82, **81, 82, 83,** 83–84

lack of air combat training 37, 48
Lesan, Capt Thomas 75–76, **76**
losses 14, 23, 25, 27, 28, 35, 39, 45, 49, 50, 61, 62, 91
losses inflicted on VPAF May-June 1967 77–84, **80, 83, 86**
Lufbery circle, the 33, 67, 79

manoeuvrability 7, 14, 15, 40, 45
medals and awards **9,** 63, 65, 70, **86, 89, 91**
MER (multiple ejector rack) 7
MiGCAP missions 64, 69, 77, 81, 84, 85, 86, 88, 91
missile performance 13–14
missiles 18; AA-2A (K-13) 'Atoll' missiles (USSR) 14, 30, 32, 45, 47, 49, 64–65, 75, 85, **88;** AGM-45 Shrike anti-radiation missile 36, 40, 65, **89;** AIM-9B Sidewinder missiles 6, 8, 12–14, 27, 32, **33,** 34, **34,** 35, 47, 62, 68, 69, 71, 72, 74, **77,** 78, 79, **80,** 81, 82, 85, **86;** AIM-9E Sidewinder missiles 14, 45; AGM-12B Bullpup missile **7;** M61A1 Vulcan gun **10,** 10–12, **11, 12,** 34, **34;** N-37D cannon (USSR) 17, **17,** 29, 35; NR-23 cannon (USSR) 17, **17,** 29, 35
mission tours 91
movement of 'bombing line' southward 90–91

NASARR (North American Search and Ranging Radar System) 8
near misses 31–32
nicknames **22, 64, 86, 87, 89**

objectives of VPAF fighters 25, **25**
Olds, Col Robin 20, 61, 85
omission of crew names 26
Operations: *Linebacker I/II* (May-Oct 1972) 14; *Rolling Thunder* (March 1965-November 1968) 13, 22, 27, 32, 39, 90

'Pardo's Push' recovery operation 64
Phuc Yen airfield attack 86–87
pilot's weight and gear **21**
pod flying formations 44–45
POL (petrol, oil and lubricant sites) attacks 28–29, 35, 36, 45, 46, 49, 62
Pratt & Whitney J75 engine 6
procedure to follow in the event of a MiG attack 24
Project *Feather Duster* 16
Project *Have Doughnut* 19
prototypes 6

QRC-160 ECM (electronic countermeasures) pod **44,** 44–45, 61, 85

radar systems **8,** 8–9, **18,** 21, 23, 84; RP-5 Izumrud gun-aiming radar 35
rate of fire 17, 18
rate of turn 10, 68, **82**
'Rattler' strike mission on rail transportation 75–76
reconnaissance missions 20, 46, 87
repairs to gun systems 12
Republic F-105 Thunderchief fighter-bomber plane 6, 25, **27, 63,** 76; F-105B 6, **7,** 8, 9; F-105D **3,** 8–9, **11, 18,** 22, 26, 28, **28, 35,** 41, 46, 61, 74, 77; 58-1151 7; 58-1156 29, **29, 51,** 93; 58-1168 **52, 67, 68,** 93; 59-1725 50; 59-1754 23; 59-1755 33; 59-1766 **59,** 95; 59-1772 **53,** 64, **73,** 93; 60-0415 **57,** 94; 60-0424 **55, 81, 82, 86,** 94; 60-0447 **27;** 60-0458 36, **59,** 95; 60-0490 **8;** 60-0497 **55, 77,** 94; 60-0498 **53,** 76, 93; 60-0501 **59,** 95; 60-0504 **58, 74,** 95; 60-0505 **22;** 60-0518 **49;** 60-0522 **57, 80,** 94; 60-5376 **88;** 61-0069 **55, 60, 83,** 94, 95; 61-0105 **7;** 61-0109 **51, 64,** 93; 61-0121 32; 61-0132 **55, 86,** 94; 61-0136 **54,** 94; 61-0159 **54, 60,** 93, 95; 61-0198 **44;** 61-0220 **47;** 62-480 39; 62-4231 **7;** 62-4262 **54,** 94; 62-4278 **51,** 93; 62-4284 **7, 56, 58, 87,** 94, 95; 62-4294 73; 62-4301 **45, 60,** 95; 62-4306 38; 62-4334 **42;** 62-4347 **70;** 62-4364 **52,** 93; 62-4384 **53, 69,** 93; 62-4394 **58,** 95; F-105F 9, 11, 25, 30, 36; 63-8267 **66–67;** 63-8272 **66–67;** 63-8301 **9, 52,** 93; 63-8317 **57, 89, 91,** 94; 63-8320 90, **90;** 63-8329 **56,** 94; 63-8341 65–66; F-105F *Wild Weasels* 27, 73, 74, 91
RESCAP (rescue combat air patrol) 26, 35, 66–67, 70–71, 75
Richter, Lt Karl **40,** 41, **41, 42, 43**
Rilling, Maj Robert 72, 79, 80, **80**
Robinson, Maj William P. 40
RoE (Rules of Engagement) **43**
Route Pack VIA 34, 91

SAM suppression missions 28, 31, 36, 41, 63–64, 66–68, **67**
SAMs (surface to air missiles) 27, 29, 44, 45, 65, **67,** 80, 88
Scott, Col Robert R **7,** 64, **64,** 65
Seaver, Maj 'Mo' **77,** 78, **79, 80,** 83
Snakeye ordnance **82**
Soviet assistance 19–20
split-S manoeuvre 39
strike training 21–22

testing projects 19
Thai Nguyen attacks 35, 62
Thorsness, Maj Leo K 4, 65, 66, **66,** 67, 70, 75
'Thud Ridge' mountain range 31, 32, 37, 45, 50, 72, 75, 78, 79, 85
Tolman, Maj Fred 68–69, **69**
Tracy, Maj Fred 29, **29**
training **9,** 10, 16, 19, 20–22, 37, 91

US acquisition of MiGs 19
USAF: 4520th Combat Crew Training Wing 9, **59,** 95; TFS (Tactical Fighter Squadron): 34th 85, 94; 333rd 35, **35,** 64, 77; 354th **63, 68, 69,** 86; 433rd 77; TFW (Tactical Fighter Wing): 4th **7,** 8, **74;** 8th 14, 61, 64, 85, 86; 18th **7,** 20, **74;** 23rd **7,** 20, **27,** 74; 36th **8, 9, 9, 59, 74,** 95; 44th **21;** 49th **8;** 354th 22, 28, 50, **54;** 355th **8, 9,** 17, 20, 23, 31, 33, 45, 46, **51, 52–54, 56, 57–58,** 61, **62,** 64, 65, **65, 66,** 72, 74–75, 78, 86, 88, 93, 94, 95; 366th 81, 86; 388th 6, 20, 24, 28, 29, 30, 37, 39, 43, 45, **51, 55, 59, 61,** 62, **79,** 86, **88,** 93, 94, 95; 416th 23; 419th **60,** 95; 474th 46; 6441st 20

VPAF (Vietnamese People's Air Force) 14, 17, 19–20, 25, 27, 45, **49,** 84; 921st FR 20, 22, 61; 923rd FR 20, **28,** 33; tactics 30, 31, 32, 34, 36, 44, 45, 61, 85, 88, 91

weaknesses of the F-105 16, 30, 31, 37, **43,** 45, **49,** 50, 62, 63
weapons delivery avionics 8
weight 6
Wheeler, Maj William 89, **89, 90, 91**
Wiggins, Capt Larry D 81–82, **82, 83**
Wild Weasel missions **9, 27,** 36, 61, 65, 87
Wilson, Lt Fred A. 42, **42–43**
wing tanks 43

Xuan Mai army barracks attack 65–68

'Zinc' flight of USAF TFS 22–23